TOKUSATSU, TRANSMUTATIONS, AND TITANS

AN A-Z GUIDE TO JAPANESE SCI-FI FILMS

George Cervenka Jr.

fineline **press**
reminderville, ohio

Tokusatsu, Transmutations, and Titans:
An A-Z Guide to Japanese Sci-Fi Films

Edited by Kerry Rudy

Printed by 48HrBooks
Akron, Ohio
www.48HrBooks.com

Contents

Intro 5
A Guide To The Guide 7
(Not Your Typical) Ratings System 9
A-Z Film Reviews 11
Talk The Talk 143

Intro

Sometimes my loving wife looks at me kinda funny. Why is a sports-minded family man in his early 50s ardently watching an overgrown, irradiated lizard lay waste to Tokyo? Or better yet, finding delight at the sight of a giant, tusky turtle spinning high in the air like a wobbly Frisbee fling? As odd as it may seem, I've always found Japanese science-fiction cinema to be a wonderfully absurd and strangely-intoxicating diversion. The upshot is this handy-dandy little guide, featuring "mini-reviews" of 176 movies viewed over a three-year span.

But, alas, these fanciful films are often easy targets for scorn. This is, after all, a genre characterized by full-grown men donning rubber costumes and whacking the poop out of each other. And, yeah, sometimes the miniature flying saucers, cars, jets, helicopters, and tanks – especially the tanks – are undeniably toylike. Misaligned dubbing and puzzling editing choices from American movie distributors certainly haven't helped.

To all this I say . . . so what?

Despite the occasional view of the wires suspending the majestic moth Mothra or the testy pterosaur Rodan, these misunderstood flicks are often cleverly creative and innovative. The special effects work is frequently stellar, especially when one considers that the filmmakers constantly dealt with low budgets and strict deadlines.

We need to take a closer look.

Pick up a copy of G-Fan, North America's premiere fanzine of Godzilla and all things related, or attend the annual G-Fest convention in Chicago, and you might be amazed at the fervor surrounding this unique cinematic phenomenon. And the love is passed down to a younger generation of fans. My daughters – ages 16 and 19 – can easily rattle off their favorite daikaiju ("giant monster") or tokusatsu ("special effects") films.

I was lucky to grow up during the heyday of Cleveland, Ohio creature feature television hosts. The 1970s saw Hoolihan and Big Chuck (later Big Chuck and Lil' John), Super Host, and the Ghoul combine to offer a steady stream of Far East fantasy flicks interspersed amongst their weekly sci-fi and horror movie presentations. The Ghoul (inspired by the legendary Ghoulardi) even added sound effects, music, and other audio inserts to the film's soundtrack, with Godzilla, for example, letting out a full-bodied belch after every blast of his atomic heat ray. And, instead of tribal drums, the natives of Mothra's Infant Island gyrated and swayed during their sacred dance ritual to a polka tune!

So join me, if you will, on a mission to enlighten and, hopefully, amuse. Despite the four-star ratings system used in this book, I've never really watched Japanese sci-fi with much of a critical eye. So don't expect to find cheap shots or vicious diatribes. Warts and all, these films are flat-out fun. And maybe . . . just maybe . . . the uninitiated will see they've been given a bum rap.

--George Cervenka Jr.

A Guide To The Guide

Soon into the start of this book I realized I had to lay down a few ground rules. Sure, the Godzilla flicks and the like were no-brainers for inclusion. But what about those films that are on the fringe? Often, a movie of a different genre – a horror pic, for instance – will contain a sci-fi twist crucial to the plot. So, after much contemplation, here is my criteria:

*The films reviewed in this guide must have a sci-fi element important to the story, even if predominantly belonging to another genre. Hence, you'll notice horror, fantasy, and spy pictures also gracing these pages. As long as some sci-fi is involved, they're included.

*The film must have seen some sort of U.S. release (theater, film fest, or home version) even if on a limited basis.

*Movies with minimal creative input from Japanese production companies were not critiqued. Such films include THE BERMUDA DEPTHS, THE IVORY APE, and SOLAR CRISIS. Japanese participation in these pics was primarily needed for funding purposes.

Note: One of the quandaries facing the newbie Japanese sci-fi fan is the confounding number of alternate titles bestowed upon films. Foreign movies were often released stateside with "U.S. marketable" names. I'm partial to the monikers of my youth. Therefore, the film currently recognized as MOTHRA VS. GODZILLA is listed in this guide under its original American title, GODZILLA VS. THE THING. Alternate titles, however, are conveniently cross-referenced.

The reviews in this book contain several abbreviations. Here's a succinct synopsis:

J (followed by year): Japanese year of release
US (followed by year): United States year of release
AKA (Also Known As): the movie's alternate title(s)
D: Director
C: Cast

The film's production company appears in uppercase at the end of the review. All films are in color unless stated otherwise in the body of the review.

(Not Your Typical) Ratings System

I must confess that I get a major kick out of just about all of the far-out flicks commonly associated with the wild world of Japanese science-fiction cinema. Thus, the ratings system below tends to be far more generous, I'm sure, than that of your average reviewer. With that in mind . . .

****	A must-see for serious genre fans
***	Highly-recommended watch
**	Only devout fans will want to see it
*	So bad it's good

Note: In recent years, quite a few of the original Japanese versions of the movies in this guide have been released with English subtitles. Free of the awkward dubbing and disconcerting editing decisions that hampered their U.S. presentations, most of these films – when seen as initially intended – are decidedly better. Notable examples, such as GOJIRA, the Japanese source of GODZILLA, KING OF THE MONSTERS, are referenced when merited.

A

ALIEN VS. NINJA (J 2010, US 2010) ** Not a bad idea, eh? Stealthy, lightning-quick aliens taking on energetic, katana-wielding ninja. This one, however, might not be what you'd expect. It's another in a slew of outrageous sci-fi films from Japan steeped in blood, gore, and dismemberment. A notorious ninja clan witnesses a giant fireball crash into the woods near their village. They investigate and discover a rabble of rubbery reptilian extraterrestrials who happen to find ninja meat rather savory. The opposing factions square off in a muddle of preposterous skirmishes. Sure, there's some nifty ninja swordplay, but our alien invaders here look pretty goofy. That's probably by design, but I can't help thinking what a cool flick this could have been if played in a serious vein. Connoisseurs of camp, though, will undoubtedly dig it. AKA: AVN: ALIEN VS. NINJA. D: Seiji Chiba. C: Masinori Mimoto, Shuji Kashiwabara, Miki Higii, Donpei Tsuchihira. NIKKATSU/SUSHI TYPHOON/NORTH CRY

ALIVE (J 2002, US 2004) **½ Carefully-paced mindbender about a death-row inmate (Hideo Sakaki) who survives his execution attempt and faces a choice: get refried in the electric chair – or take part in a series of unusual, dangerous scientific experiments. He opts for the latter and is placed in a spacious underground prison cell with a demented rapist and a mysterious young woman infected with an alien parasite. Said parasite, referred to as an "isomer," empowers its host with a bevy of supernatural abilities – a development that catches the attention of the Japanese military. Their involvement shifts the film into a higher gear. A surprisingly restrained offering from Ryuhei Kitamura, the creative force behind VERSUS and GODZILLA: FINAL WARS. Expect only a couple of the director's customary frenetic fight scenes. The finale, nonetheless, is a real doozy. D: Kitamura. C: Sakaki, Ryo, Koyuki, Shun Sagata, Erika Oda, Tak Sakaguchi. NAPALM/SUPLEX

ALL MONSTERS ATTACK See GODZILLA'S REVENGE

ANDROMEDIA (J 1998, US 2004) **½ An atypical production from maverick filmmaker Takashi Miike, ANDROMEDIA is not only a sci-fi thriller but a vehicle to showcase the sugar-coated appeal of the female J-pop quartet, SPEED. When teenager Mai (Hiroko Shimabukuro) dies in a traffic mishap, her scientist father converts her logged memories into a cyberspace replication known as Ai. Amazingly, Ai mirrors Mai's appearance and playful personality. She even hangs out with Mai's schoolgal pals by way of laptop computer. The old boyfriend? He's also back in the picture – and still smitten. A shady organization tries to swipe the groundbreaking technology, and the chase is on. Strange, strange moment: Da Pump, the Japanese equivalent of New Kids On The Block, arrives on the scene – presumably to help – but instead launches into a tightly-choreographed, MTV-style music video. Miike is unpredictable, but who could have seen *that* coming? Without doubt, though, a respectable little effort. D: Miike. C: SPEED (Shimabukuro, Eriko Imai, Takako Uehara, Hitoe Araki), Kenji Harada. AVEX/EXCELLENT FILM/SEDIC INTERNATIONAL/TOKYO BROADCASTING SYSTEM

ASSAULT GIRLS (J 2009, US 2010) **½ Though I don't know many of their ilk, I'm guessing hardcore gamers will appreciate the novelty of ASSAULT GIRLS. It's not so much a flick as it is a drop-in visit to a video game in progress, as a trio of heavily-armed, leather-adorned lasses hunt down giant, wormlike creatures in a simulated desert world. Director Mamoru Oshii explored similar territory in AVALON, a 2001 film where the line between reality and virtual reality becomes gradually blurred. Things aren't nearly as drastic here, as "offed" players can re-enter the game. Dialogue is sparse, with emphasis placed on Oshii's inclination toward measured pacing and salient visuals. CGI mayhem, however, is in abundance. Those who favor a standard Hollywood approach to their sci-fi could very well find themselves exasperated. Rinko Kikuchi (PACIFIC RIM) portrays one of the assault gals. D: Oshii. C: Meisa Kuroki, Kikuchi, Hinako Saeki, Yoshikazu Fujiki. DEIZ/GENEON UNIVERSAL ENTERTAINMENT

ATOMIC RULERS See ATOMIC RULERS OF THE WORLD

ATOMIC RULERS OF THE WORLD (J 1957, US 1964) ** The first of four mind-boggling flicks to feature Starman, the Japanese answer, of sorts, to Superman. The celestial superhero (clad in an ill-fitting white bodysuit) is sent to Earth by the High Council of the Emerald Planet to prevent an impending nuclear holocaust planned by the country of Magolia. Resistant to bullets and endowed with super strength, Starman – played with a wink and a nod by Ken Utsui – effortlessly sheds a throng of Magolian aggressors. Not that he needs it, but an impressionable group of school-aged orphans offer assistance. Pieced together from the SUPER GIANT series of short films popular in Japan, there's action aplenty, albeit it in glorious black-and-white. AKA: ATOMIC RULERS. D: Teruo Ishii, Akira Mitsuwa, Koreyoshi Akasaka. C: Utsui, Junko Ikeuchi. FUJI/SHINTOHO

ATRAGON (J 1963, US 1965) ***½ Splendiferous sci-fi adventure from Toho's golden era, with director Ishiro Honda and special effects man Eiji Tsuburaya at the height of their creative powers. The undersea inhabitants of the vaunted Mu Empire resurface after 12,000 years to reclaim their rule on the mainland. Desperate for help, Japanese officials seek out the legendary Captain Jinguchi, a long-lost naval commander hiding out on a tranquil tropical isle in the Pacific. Jinguchi (stoically played by Jun Tazaki) has designed a flying super sub, the Atragon. This red-and-silver beauty, equipped with a spiffy drill nose and a potent freeze cannon, can travel by land, water, air - even underground! The Muans counter by unleashing Manda, a serpentine dragon added to the film for box-office appeal. Shinichi Sekizawa's script zips steadily along, and the well-versed cast settles easily into their roles. Kenji Sahara is especially interesting as a nonconventional news reporter. Akira Ifukube's stirring score adeptly hits all the right accent points. Based on a run of novels by Shunro Ishikawa, the Jules Verne of Japan. D: Honda. C: Tadao Takashima, Yoko Fujiyama, Yu Fujiki, Sahara, Ken Uehara. TOHO

ATTACK FROM SPACE (J 1957-58, US 1964) *½ Starman, the interplanetary superhero in the tightie whities, returns to defend Earth in this third of four films adapted for American audiences from the SUPER GIANT movie series. This time, it's nasty aliens from the Sapphire Galaxy threatening to nuke us, and they're brainwashing our top scientific geniuses into blind submission. Never fear, Starman is here! Our brawny, yet limber, protagonist laughs with delight as he puts a serious whuppin' on the extraterrrestrial bad boys. Fans of low-budget cinema seem to truly relish the Starman pics. They're out-and-out goofy. Luckily, an attentive narrator occasionally jumps in to explain what the frig is goin' on. Left unanswered, however, is a scene where plain folk subsist in interstellar space without the use of oxygen tanks or spacesuits. You gotta love this stuff! For those who need to know, it's presented in stark black-and-white. D: Teruo Ishii, Akira Mitsuwa, Koreyoshi Akasaka. C: Ken Utsui, Junko Ikeuchi. FUJI/SHINTOHO

ATTACK OF THE MONSTERS (J 1969, US 1969) *** Possibly Gamera's wildest ride as director Noriaki Yuasa and writer Fumi Takahashi pull out all the stops in the humongous flying turtle's fifth outing. A pair of intrepid schoolboys discover an unoccupied spacecraft in the Japanese countryside. Naturally, they hop aboard, and are soon whisked to a planet inhabited by two brain-eating space chicks. Gamera, friend to all children, comes to the rescue. But check this out: The alien base is guarded by the knife-headed Guiron, who would love nothing better than to slice, dice, and chop our reptile pal into tasty turtle nuggets. Guiron, an unusual rhino/shark crossbreed, also has the ability to discharge skin-piercing ninja stars! Amid the lively sparring, an acrobatic Gamera impresses with a well-executed gymnastics routine. See the Japanese version (or the GAMERA VS. GUIRON release by Sandy Frank) for one of the more outlandish encounters in daikaiju eiga history. Space Gyaos (the chiropteran creature from RETURN OF THE GIANT MONSTERS, covered here with silver spray paint) pops in for a visit and has its limbs severed, one-at-a-time, by Guiron's steely head blade! AKA: GAMERA VS. GUIRON. D: Yuasa. C: Nobuhiro Kajima, Christopher Murphy, Miyuki Akiyama, Kon Omura. DAIEI

ATTACK OF THE MUSHROOM PEOPLE (J 1963, US 1965) **** The title automatically gets a hearty chuckle, but don't be fooled. This engrossing chiller is arguably the iconic director Ishiro Honda's best film. A luxury yacht sails into a horrendous storm, stranding the seven passengers on a fog-ladened South Pacific island. The resourceful castaways find refuge in a fungus-infested ship anchored offshore; its crew, studying the effects of nuclear radiation, is nowhere in sight. The ship's log warns against consuming the mushrooms originating from the island, for they severely damage human nerve tissue. With their food supply rapidly dwindling, will our desperate survivors succumb to the allure of the tempting shrooms? The superb ensemble cast, featuring some of Toho's finest, act their arses off. And Hajime Koizumi's cinematography is mesmerizing. Worst suspicions are confirmed when a few of the research ship's missing crew turn up as mobile mushroom creatures. Well, you know, you are what you eat . . . AKA: MATANGO. D: Honda. C: Akira Kubo, Kumi Mizuno, Kenji Sahara, Hiroshi Koizumi, Yoshio Tsuchiya. TOHO

ATTACK OF THE SUPER MONSTERS, THE (J 1977-78, US 1982) * An inexplicable combination of animation, puppetry, and suitmation clash in this mind-warping experiment from the twisted think tank at Tsuburaya Productions. It's the year 2000, and dinosaurs (trash-talking ones, no less!) have reappeared after centuries of cavern-dwelling beneath Earth's surface. Emperor Tyrannus, a grouchy T-Rex, telepathically orders his prehistoric kith to go on the offensive. The four-person Gemini Force, in an Atragon-inspired flying combat vehicle, is called forth to investigate matters. The transitions from the crew's animated sequences to the live-action monster scenes are, to put it mildly, quite jarring. Edited together from the first four episodes of a Japanese TV series, some will find this fractured flick good for a laugh or two. Choose to be amused, I say. D: Toru Sotogama, Hiroshi Jinzeni. C: Tom Wyner (voice). TSUBURAYA PRODUCTIONS

ATTACK ON TITAN: END OF THE WORLD (J 2015, US 2015) **½ As the result of a unique marketing strategy, this follow-up flick to ATTACK ON TITAN: PART ONE appeared in Japanese theaters within two months of the release of its predecessor. Young buck Eren Yeager and the rest of the Scouting Regimen are still battling the Titans, goofy-faced giants who ingest humans. Part of the perverse draw of TITAN, for many, is the horrifying depiction of folks getting torn apart limb-by-limb, swallowed whole, or bitten in half – with the resultant splash of blood. This entry focuses more on the conflict between a newer form of Titans, who seem to possess intelligence and are mighty powerful. Eren, without giving away too much, figures prominently. Fierce CGI tussles ensue, with the fate of civilization hanging in the balance. Toho brass took note of director Shinji Higuchi's work in the TITAN pics and entrusted him with the task of co-directing SHIN GODZILLA. AKA: ATTACK ON TITAN: PART TWO. D: Higuchi. C: Haruma Miura, Kiko Mizuhara, Kanata Hongo, Hiroki Hasegawa, Satomi Ishihara. TOHO/KODANSHA/LICRI/NIKKATSU

ATTACK ON TITAN: PART ONE (J 2015, US 2015) *** The Attack on Titan franchise is, as they say, "big in Japan." Hajime Isayama's much-read manga has inspired an anime series, video games, novels, merchandise tie-ins – and finally – a pair of highly-anticipated live-action motion pics. Part one (of a duology) gets right to it: A century has passed since the Titans, a horde of naked, people-eating giants without reproductive organs, devoured most of mankind. Massive walls now surround an agrarian-based expanse of land in Japan, and peace prevails. Youthful Eren Yeager, along with friends Mikasa and Armin, yearn to see the outside world. They even doubt that the Titans still exist when, right on cue, the biggest and baddest Titan ever known smashes through a section of the wall. A multitude of Titans rush in, hand-picking the panic-stricken locals one-by-one and gobbling 'em down like convenient snack treats. The region is practically wiped out. A couple of years go by, and Eren (and his cohorts) have reemerged – thanks to intense training – as tether-swinging, sword-slashing swashbucklers with the skills to attack the Titans' only vulnerable spot: the nape of the neck. Plenty of thrills and (blood) spills follow. Director Shinji Higuchi (JAPAN SINKS, SHIN GODZILLA) guided the film to the 17th-highest gross of the year in Japan. The sequel, ATTACK ON TITAN: END OF THE WORLD, would show up in theaters a mere month-and-a-half later. D: Higuchi. C: Haruma Miura, Kiko Mizuhara, Satomi Ishihara, Kanata Hongo,

Hiroki Hasegawa, Nanami Sakuraba. TOHO/ KODANSHA/ LICRI/NIKKATSU

ATTACK ON TITAN: PART TWO See ATTACK ON TITAN: END OF THE WORLD

AVALON (J 2001, POLAND 2002, US 2003) *** Talk about an unlikely pairing. AVALON was filmed in Europe with a Polish cast by noted director Mamoru Oshii and a Japanese production team. It's an odd melding of cultures, for sure, but it clicks. Our story takes place in the near future, where a significant portion of the populace is addicted to an illegal, virtual-reality war game. Problem is, an increasing number of participants end up brain-dead while attempting to access the game's highest level, thought by some to be unattainable. Expert gamer Ash (Malgorzata Foremniak) welcomes the challenge. Possessing an ice-cold glare and plenty of moxie, she's the kind of gal you wouldn't want to bet against. But is this an unwinnable game? The film is moderately paced – an Oshii trademark – with fastidious attention accorded to even the most minor of details. That's not to imply there's a lack of get-up-and-go; it just comes in flourishes. And the extensive use of computer-generated special effects makes perfect sense. A majority of the pic is lensed in an orangish hue, lending a glum, ominous feel to the proceedings. Oshii, incidentally, helmed the anime classic, GHOST IN THE SHELL, but is equally effective with live-action fare. D: Oshii. C: Foremniak, Wladyslaw Kowalski, Jerzy Gudejko, Dariusz Biskupski, Bartek Swiderski. DEIZ

AVN: ALIEN VS. NINJA See ALIEN VS. NINJA

B

BATTLE IN OUTER SPACE (J 1959, US 1960) ***½ Made during the early days of the Space Race – when we weren't exactly sure what lurked above – this Toho tokusatsu tour de force resonates with a warm, wonderful retro feel. The second film of director Ishiro Honda's acclaimed outer space trilogy, BATTLE IN OUTER SPACE is highly-imaginative, visually stunning, and loaded to the brim with intricate miniatures, extravagant sets, and vivid special effects. Alien intruders cause mucho trouble on Earth, prompting world leaders to dispatch a pair of manned rocketships to the moon to destroy their base of operations. A cosmic confrontation with flying saucers ensues, with profuse amounts of laser fire and explosions. The conflict continues on our terrain when remote-controlled meteors strike Manhattan and the Golden Gate Bridge. Of course, Tokyo is not spared; in one of SFX pioneer Eiji Tsuburaya's "loftiest" moments, a good chunk of the city is literally sucked into the air by the extraterrestrials' anti-gravity beam. Rare for a Toho sci-fi flick in that there is nary a kaiju. However, the pygmy-sized aliens, squeaking like a litter of newborn pups, are strange enough. D: Honda. C: Ryo Ikebe, Kyoko Anzai, Minoru Takada, Koreya Senda, Yoshio Tsuchiya. TOHO

BIG MAN JAPAN (J 2007, US 2008) ***½ Japanese comedian Hitoshi Matsumoto directed, co-wrote, and starred in this offbeat mockumentary about a middle-aged loner – dubbed "Big Sato" – who transforms into a 100-foot-high, mammoth-haired sumo warrior to protect Japan from giant monsters. The last of his kind, our low-key "hero" is underappreciated and even hated by the masses, who feel he does more harm than good. Sato is summoned by the Department of Defense to neutralize a legion of sizeable CGI oddities. Among 'em: the Strangling Monster, which uproots skyscrapers with its fantastic, elastic limbs; the Leaping Monster (basically, a hop-happy foot); the Stink Monster, which emits a foul odor 10,000 times stronger than normal human feces; and the Evil Stare Monster (a projectile eyeball). A humorous flick, for certain, yet somewhat somber and thought-provoking. Sato's wife and child, embarrassed by his line of work, have abandoned him. And frankly, the pay could be much better. Deliberately paced, an abrupt twist near film's end may baffle the viewer. Nonetheless, this is inspired work. D: Matsumoto. C: Matsumoto, Riki Takeuchi, Ua. PHANTOM FILM/REAL PRODUCT/SHOCHIKU/YOSHIMOTO/KAGYO

BLOOD TYPE: BLUE (J 1978, US 1979) *½ A real bummer of a flick. UFOs start appearing all over the world, and the folks who see 'em find their blood has turned blue. The neophyte blood types, despite no apparent threat, are quickly targeted. Governments around the globe reveal their prejudices, and military muscle is utilized. Those who hang in there 'til the bitter end are bound to be disheartened. And the UFOs? We're only privy to newspaper accounts. You gotta figure that Toho surely had a stockpile of flying saucers gathering dust in the prop room, right? Consequently, there's a lot of heavy-duty drama going down in this one. Rarely seen in the States, especially nowadays. AKA: BLUE CHRISTMAS. D: Kihachi Okamoto. C: Hiroshi Katsuno, Eiji Okada, Keiko Takashita, Kaoru Yachigusa, Masaya Oki. TOHO

BLUE CHRISTMAS See BLOOD TYPE: BLUE

BODY SNATCHER FROM HELL See GOKE, BODYSNATCHER FROM HELL

C

CASSHERN (J 2004, US 2007) *** Futuristic thriller employing the digital backlot process that distinguished such flicks as SKY CAPTAIN AND THE WORLD OF TOMORROW and SIN CITY. The actors are filmed in front of a green screen, with the background added digitally in post-production. The result is often an otherworldly feel; CASSHERN is no exception. It's the late 21st century and war has left Earth in a mire of disease and pollution. A regenerative treatment developed by a renowned scientist is the only hope for a dying human race. Complications arise, and a horde of mutant creatures emerge. They pal up with an army of imposing robots to wreak serious havoc. Enter the mighty Casshern, a reanimated soldier shielded by indestructible protective clothing and possessing superhuman abilities. Stay on the alert, as the action is frantic. Director Kazuaki Kiriya captures the spirit of the early 1970s anime off which the pic is based. Besides the optical indulgence, there's a cool soundtrack to boot. D: Kiriya. C: Yusuke Iseya, Kumiko Aso, Akira Terao, Kanako Higuchi. SHOCHIKU

CATASTROPHE: 1999 See PROPHECIES OF NOSTRADAMUS

CLONE RETURNS HOME, THE (J 2008, US 2008) ***½ What becomes of the soul when someone is cloned? That's the heady question posed in this pensive, heart-wrenching sci-fi drama that caught the attention of filmgoers at the 2009 Sundance Film Festival. An astronaut (Mitsuhiro Oikawa) dies during an outer space mission and is replaced back on Earth by his clone. Things aren't quite kosher, though, as the clone's memory is fixated on a tragic event from the late astronaut's childhood. Seeking solace, he escapes from the lab and wanders about Japan's rural environs. Writer and director Kanji Nakajima steers the story with a steady hand, deftly examining the moral ramifications of human duplication. Those looking for a "pick-me-up" type of flick, however, should search elsewhere. This tale is just so dang sad. D: Nakajima. C: Oikawa, Eri Ishida, Hiromi Nagasaku, Kyusaku Shimada, Toru Shinagawa. ANIMEIGO/THE CLONE RETURNS HOME FILM PARTNERS

CUTIE HONEY (J 2004, US 2007) **** The hectic pace, upbeat demeanor, and wild exaggeration of "magical girl" anime and manga is shamelessly flaunted in this live-action adventure featuring the free-spirited superheroine known as Cutie Honey. Adorable, bubbly office worker Honey Kisaragi (Eriko Sato) changes into the pink-swathed, fuchsia-coiffed "warrior of love" to thwart the evil Panther Claw organization from stealing the powerful I-system, a device conceived by Honey's prof father for the purpose of sustaining her life. Sato is perfectly cast as the cheerful, mischievous Honey; she's incredibly confident yet vulnerable. Sure, this is silly fun, carried to the hilt. But it all falls nicely into place. Amid a constant flow of J-pop music, director Hideaki Anno (EVANGELION) maintains a brisk tempo. Created by Go Nagai in the early 1970's, CUTIE HONEY undoubtedly paved the way for the Sailor Moon mania that would later hit U.S. shores. D: Anno. C: Sato, Mikako Ichikawa, Jun Murakami. GAINAX/WOWOW

CYBER NINJA (J 1988, US 1994) ** The sheer audacity of CYBER NINJA – a film set in the distant future in what appears to be feudal Japan – may leave some mystified. But the pic certainly has its appeal. Keita Amemiya's first theatrical release is chock-full of the energetic action sequences and colorful visual effects that would typify the inventive director's later fare (which includes the ZEIRAM movies, MOON OVER TAO, and MECHANICAL VIOLATOR HAKAIDER). When a princess from the Suwabeh clan is abducted by an intergalactic malefactor, a small group of loyal followers set out to rescue her. They're joined by our title character: a warrior believed dead but reborn as a fleet, bionic fighting machine. A flurry of sword-swingin' and laser-zingin' ensues, in a far-out fable that includes technologically-enhanced ninjas and flying fortresses amongst its delights. Though often hard to grasp, it's evident that this is the work of a young filmmaker with immense promise. D: Amemiya. C: Hanbei Kawai, Hiroki Ida, Eri Morishita, Makoto Yokoyama, Fuyukichi Maki. CROWD/NAMCO

D

DAGORA, THE SPACE MONSTER (J 1964, US 1965) ***1/2 Enjoyable jewel heist whodunit with plenty of kaiju quirkiness. Diamonds are disappearing around the world at an alarming rate. The culprit is found to be a big ol' jellyfish, formed when space cells are mutated by radiation in Earth's atmosphere. Hovering in the clouds, the tentacled terror has a craving for carbon-based matter, sucking up not only diamonds, but mass hauls of coal. As Japan's brightest scientists race to find a solution, a wiseacre detective (played by Robert Dunham) is hot on the trail of a hardened gang of jewel thieves. Dunham (sometimes billed as Dan Yuma) has fun with the character; it's unfortunate he didn't get more high-profile "gaikokujin" roles as he was fluent in Japanese. It's interesting to note that Dagora, the giant jellyfish, was not depicted by a guy in a monster suit. Rather, the effect was achieved through a combination of puppetry and cartoon animation. One of the more underrated Toho efforts. AKA: DOGORA. D: Ishiro Honda. C: Yosuke Natsuki, Dunham, Akiko Wakabayashi, Yoko Fujiyama, Hiroshi Koizumi. TOHO

DAIMAJIN See MAJIN, MONSTER OF TERROR

DAIMAJIN STRIKES AGAIN See MAJIN STRIKES AGAIN

DARK SOLDIER D (J 1998, US 2001) ** Whoa. Is that an oversized rubber chicken running amok? Yep, sure looks like it, and the 50-foot-tall featherless fiend is in a *fowl* mood as well. We're only halfway through this deranged flick and well over 100 of the humans have been consumed by the big bird. Blame it on the fluorescent green goop seeping from a batch of recently-fallen meteorites; the syrupy substance attaches itself to living hosts to create nightmarish monstrosities. To the rescue is Kawamata, a heartless mercenary, and his copter-flying sidekick, Matsuzaki. The detestable duo, prone to macho posturing and fits of maniacal laughter, filch a state-of-the-art mobile combat suit from Russian Special Operations Forces and sneak back to Japan. With a giant reptilian creature and a modest-sized motorized spider on the loose, Kawamata dons the robotic rig to test his mettle. The result: a fair amount of blood, guts, and mutilated body parts. The use of high-definition video (though possibly cost-driven) suggests that DARK SOLDIER D was originally meant as a television project. In fact, the film is comprised of three half-hour "mini-movies," which can be viewed separately – or together – and still remain intelligible. D: Nobuya Okabe. C: Daisuke Nagakura, Masanori Machida. BUILDUP ENTERTAINMENT

DAY OF RESURRECTION See VIRUS

DEAD OR ALIVE: FINAL (J 2002, US 2002) ** ½ The third film in anarchic director Takashi Miike's DEAD OR ALIVE trilogy unexpectedly transports us from the modern-day yakuza milieu of the series' first two outings and straight into the tech-driven realm of sci-fi. It's the year 2346, and a dark, direful Yokohama is ruled by a mayor who is out of his friggin' gourd. (He's systematically forcing the city's residents to take anti-fertility drugs.) An armed resistance group, determined to disrupt the mayor's grand plans, is energized when a bleached-blonde battle cyborg named Ryo joins the cause. Ryo (portrayed by Show Aikawa, the principal player in Miike's ZEBRAMAN flicks) is a mellow, easy-going kind of fella – unless provoked. And that's exactly what happens when our friendly neighborhood humanoid runs into the mayor's top cop, played by a pompadoured Riki Takeuchi. The fists and feet – and bullets – start a-flyin'. The pic's riotous ending takes a strange turn, giving new meaning to the term "phallic symbol." D: Miike. C: Takeuchi, Aikawa, Josie Ho, Terence Yin, Marcia Chen, Richard Cheung. DAIEI/TOEI/EXCELLENT FILM

DEATH KAPPA (J 2010, US 2010) ** The Shinsei Era has been witness to a growing number of flicks affectionately spoofing the golden age of daikaiju and tokusatsu cinema. BIG MAN JAPAN and ZEBRAMAN offer sincere, thought-provoking approaches while films like MONSTER X STRIKES BACK: ATTACK THE G-8 SUMMIT and THE WORLD SINKS EXCEPT JAPAN are intentionally wacky. Count DEATH KAPPA among the latter, though it takes awhile to figure out this one is primarily farcical. Kanako, a young J-pop singer, humbly retreats home to her small, bucolic town when her career is quietly derailed in big-city Tokyo. When her grandmother suddenly dies, an apprehensive Kanako is left in charge of the local water spirit – a potbellied, half-shelled lizard known as Kappa. He's a peculiar little dude, with an affinity for cucumbers and Kanako's sugary-sweet timbre. When an evil faction detonates a nuclear bomb, Kappa and a fire-breathin' sea dragon named Hangyolas enlarge to gigantic proportions. An outlandish showdown ensues, with a wound-up Kappa enthusiastically exhibiting his volleyball prowess. Director Tomoo Haraguchi (MIKADROID: ROBOKILL BENEATH DISCO CLUB LAYLA) deliberately stages the special effects in a low-budget light. The miniatures are simplistic, the toy tanks are bargain-bin specials, and the wires affixed to the obligatory fighter planes are clearly visible. D: Haraguchi. C: Misato Hirata, Mika, Ryuki Kitaoka, Daniel Aguilar, Yakan Nabe. NIKKATSU/FEVER DREAMS

DEATH NOTE III See L: CHANGE THE WORLD

DEATH NOTE L: CHANGE THE WORLD See L: CHANGE THE WORLD

DEATHQUAKE (J 1980, US 1982) ** Part soap opera, part disaster flick. No one's listening when an earnest seismologist warns that an earthquake will strike Tokyo within the month. The poor guy is disowned by his family, and falls into the arms of another woman (who, in turn, already has a boyfriend). The earthquake hits, and it's a dilly. Glass shatters and buildings crumble. A slow-moving drama does an about-face as everyday folk struggle for survival amidst roaring fires and rumbling flood waters. It's darn impressive stuff from SPFX director Teruyoshi Nakano, especially the rendering of a jumbo jet crash-landing during severe seismic activity. All in all, pretty bleak, as countless numbers keel over and die. Hal Linden (yep, Barney Miller) narrates the U.S. version. AKA: EARTHQUAKE 7.9. D: Kenjiro Omori. C: Hiroshi Katsumo, Toshiyuki Nagashima, Yumi Takigawa, Kayo Matsuo, Shuji Otaki. TOHO

DEMEKING, THE SEA MONSTER (J 2009, US 2010) *** We need to get a few things straight before jumping headfirst into discourse of this misrepresented pic. For starters: Demeking, despite the film's title, is actually from outer space. The creature – a giant, flame-heavin' snail with illuminated eyeballs – does take a momentary plunge into a massive waterway, but there's little to indicate that the musky mollusk inhabits (or particularly cares for) the deep blue. Furthermore, our featured monster, as magnificent as it is, makes but a brief five-minute appearance. (It's a jam-packed five minutes, for sure, as the Big D – in a dream sequence, no less – causes major turmoil in Tokyo.) What we have here, first and foremost, is a nuanced character study of societal outcasts from a quaint Japanese village whose paths intersect. High school student Kame, an easy mark for bullies, pals around with a trio of younger lads who unconditionally idolize him. The foursome stumbles upon the hideaway of an enigmatic marine park employee named Hachiya, who informs the group he is preparing for Demeking's eventual arrival. The fate of the world, he believes, is in his very hands. Hachiya suddenly bolts, leaving his newfound acquaintances to wonder if the day of reckoning is near. Based on a 1991 manga by Takashi Imashino, this is a comfy little film, set in 1970 during Expo time. A sequel, though not in the works, could be *really* interesting. D: Kohtaro Terauchi. C: Takashi Nadagi, Kohei Kiyasu. DEMEKING PRODUCTION COMMITTEE/JOLLY ROGER

DESTROY ALL MONSTERS (J 1968, US 1969) *** Roll call! It's a daikaiju free-for-all as eleven of Toho's grandest behemoths convene is this rompin,' stompin'

Showa Era spectacle. Extraterrestrial troublemakers from the planet Kilaak manipulate Earth's mightiest monsters via remote control in a plot to rule our world. Godzilla batters the Big Apple, Rodan does a number on Moscow, and Mothra (creepy-crawly version) saunters about in Beijing. Manda (the snaky serpent from ATRAGON) slinks through London, and Gorosaurus (the jumpy lizard from KING KONG ESCAPES) noses around Paris. Also on hand: the bristly Angilas (nee Anguirus), the web-spluttering spider, Spiga, and Godzilla's thickset son, Minya. With human help, the kaiju break free of the Kilaaks' hold and, true to form, press forward for Tokyo. Don't blink or you'll miss cameos by the pudgy Baragon and the inscrutable Varan; the two surreptitiously duck out of the melee near Mt. Fuji at film's end, as the sparkly Kilaak queen (played by Kyoko Ai) enlists the services of the triple-headed outer space bully, King Ghidorah. Bring it on! D: Ishiro Honda. C: Akira Kubo, Jun Tazaki, Yukiko Kobayashi, Yoshio Tsuchiya. TOHO

DESTROY ALL PLANETS (J 1968, US 1968) *** Go, Gamera, go! The spin-dizzy giant turtle takes on the super space squid Viras, ruler of a mysterious alien race bent on colonizing Earth. The first Gamera picture unabashedly intended for the tykes, as inquisitive boy scouts Jim and Masao are held captive when the celestial baddies learn of the huge green humanitarian's fondness for children. Gamera's brain waves are scanned, and we're abruptly shown a cumbersome 20 minutes of monster battle footage from WAR OF THE MONSTERS and RETURN OF THE GIANT MONSTERS. I've heard of padding movies, but this is, well, unusual. Just how strict of a budget were we workin' with here? The Gamera flicks, after all, were Daiei's biggest yen-makers at the time. Regardless, this is a mighty fun jaunt. You've gotta see the alien invaders' rotating spaceship, a curious amalgamation of striped ping-pong balls. And the kaiju confrontation at the film's close, where the parrot-faced Viras jabs its spired head into Gamera's gut, is pure, inspired lunacy. Also, the memorable and oft-maligned Gamera theme song is heard here for the first time, but without the singing Japanese kiddos. AKA: GAMERA VS. VIRAS. D: Noriaki Yuasa. C: Kojiro Hongo, Toru Takatsuka, Carl Craig, Michiko Yaegaki. DAIEI

DEVILMAN (J 2004, US 2007) *½ Adapted from Go Nagai's well-known manga series, this live-action outing didn't sit right with steadfast fans – who were quick to voice their disapproval. The film never quite settles into a comfortable groove. When a scientific experiment in Antarctica runs amiss, a gateway to Hell is opened. A horde of demons escape, merging with humans to terrorize Earth. Meek adolescent Akira Fudo is engulfed by a demonic entity and is transformed into the winged creature known as Devilman. Fudo, though, is of strong moral fiber and fights against – rather than with – the evil forces fixed on inheriting the planet. The cup of CGI special effects runneth over in this one, and the cast seems ill at ease. Nagai, incidentally, also created the manga versions of CUTIE HONEY and MAZINGER Z. D: Hiroyuki Nasu. C: Hisato Izaki, Yusuke Izaki, Ayana Sakai, Asuka Shibuya, Riyudo Uzaki. BANDAI/DYNAMIC PRODUCTIONS/RADGAR/TV ASAHI/TOEI

DIMENSION TRAVELERS, THE (J 1998, US 1999) **½ Geez, my head is in a spin after viewing this perplexing pic. Sure wish I had paid better attention way back when in physics class. Maybe then I could comprehend this tangled tale of a pair of Japanese schoolgirls with the ability to jump back-and-forth between worlds in other dimensions. Or maybe not. Might as well just kick back, relax, and not tax the ol' cranial cavity. Typical teen Midori becomes fast friends with transfer student Mayumi, a serious sort who introduces her new pal to the wonders of dimension traveling. Midori, however, ends up in precarious contexts in these surreal, alternate ambits; she's a patient in a mental institution, then the impetus behind an underground resistance movement. Or is she simply losing her mind? Heck if I know. Nevertheless, this is a fairly decent flick. Director Kazuya Konaku would go on to helm a couple of Ultraman films that would make their way stateside: ULTRAMAN TIGA AND DYNA and ULTRAMAN GAIA: THE BATTLE IN HYPERSPACE. D: Konaku. C: Chiharu Niiyama, Yasue Satoe, Satoshi Tsumabuki, Ken Nishida. BANDAI VISUAL/KADOKAWA SHOTEN

DOGORA See DAGORA, THE SPACE MONSTER

DON'T CALL ME A CON MAN (J 1965, US 1966) ***½ It's a crime that only a few of the uproariously funny films that the Crazy Cats made for Toho in the 1960s found their way to U.S. movie houses. The Cats, a comic jazz band that first came to prominence on Japanese television, starred in a dozen amiable big-screen adventures, including this 007-inspired caper involving a contingent of Nazis attempting to restore a still-alive Adolf Hitler to power. Top cat Hitoshi Ueki discovers the bad guys' secret headquarters on a secluded South Seas island, and mayhem ensues. The appealing Ueki, deemed one of Japan's finest comedic actors, bounces happily about this breezy flick. His character constantly finds himself in perilous predicaments, but always lands on his feet. Toho tokusatsu fans should note that Eiji Tsuburaya masterminded the movie's explosive special effects. The Peanuts, who played the tiny twin fairies in MOTHRA, perform a musical number. The Cats themselves sing a song, sans instruments, at the film's conclusion. Although it's next-to-impossible to locate an English-dubbed version, you can shell out $55-$60 for the Japanese Region 2 DVD, released by Toho under its domestic title, DAIBOUKEN. Here's hoping that the Cats' enthralling body of work will soon see the light of day here in the States. AKA: DON'T CALL ME A CRIME MAN. D: Kengo Furusawa. C: The Crazy Cats (Ueki, Hajime Hana, Kei Tani, Hiroshi Inuzaka, Senri Sakurai, Eitaro Ishibashi, Shin Yasuda), Reiko Dan, Fubuki Koshiji. TOHO

DON'T CALL ME A CRIME MAN See DON'T CALL ME A CON MAN

DOOMSDAY: THE SINKING OF JAPAN (J 2006, US 2007) **½ Shinji Higuchi, the special effects practitioner of the dazzling Gamera trilogy of the 1990s, moves into the director's chair for this remake of the 1973 disaster epic, SUBMERSION OF JAPAN. As to be expected, it's a visually impressive flick. An underwater earthquake in Suruga Bay prompts scientists to predict that Japan will sink into the sea in 40 years. But guess what? They're off by about 39 years as a series of CGI-crafted quakes, volcanic eruptions, and tsunamis force the masses to flee from their homes in droves. Where the frig will everyone go? The brainy Dr. Tadokaro (Etsushi Toyokawa) has a plan . . . that's just crazy enough to work. Based on the classic book "Japan Sinks" by Sakyo Komatsu, careful focus is maintained on the heated political debate, strained human relationships, and courageous rescue efforts accompanying a major calamity. Limited showing in the U.S., though a proper DVD release is said to be in discussion. D: Higuchi. C: Tsuyoshi Kusanagi, Kou Shibasaki, Mitsuhiro Oikawa, Mayuko Fukuda, Mao Daichi. TOHO/JAPAN SINKS FILM PARTNERS

DRAGONHEAD (J 2003, US 2004) **½ Eerie, grim tale of a pair of Japanese high-schoolers who awaken from a horrific train crash only to find the planet an inhospitable wasteland. Word out amongst fellow survivors is that magnetic imbalances on Earth caused volcanoes to erupt, triggering a nuclear catastrophe. Amidst gray skies and swirling white ash, our frazzled protagonists set out for Tokyo, seeking answers. A nefarious organization called Dragonhead is believed responsible for the madness. The big draw here is the realistic post-apocalyptic scenery and gloomy atmosphere conjured up by cinematographer Junichiro Hayashi. Our main characters, a whiny guy named Teru and a hysterical gal named Ako, quickly wear out their welcome. And that's taking the whole "world in chaos" thing into account. D: Joji Iida. C: Satoshi Tsumabuki, Sayaka Kanda, Takayuki Yamada, Naohito Fujiki, Yoshimasa Kondo. TOKYO BROADCASTING SYSTEM/DRAGONHEAD FILM PARTNERS

E

EARTHQUAKE 7.9 See DEATHQUAKE

ELECTRIC DRAGON 80000V (J 2001, US 2004) **½ Raw, energetic experimental endeavor from cult filmmaker Sogo Ishii concerning a couple of intense dudes with an uncanny capacity to harness and conduct vast amounts of electricity. Zapped by heavy voltage in a childhood mishap, Dragon Eye Morrison (Tadanobu Asano) must forever endure bouts of electroshock therapy to curb a violent temper. His only salvation – besides locating lost lizards – is his electric guitar. He purposefully plugs in, cranks it to "11," and lets loose with an excess of wails and distorted riffs. Dragon Eye's nemesis is an electronics wiz with a half-metal body named Thunderbolt Buddha. Their adrenalin-fueled showdown is "jolting," to say the least. Filmed in gritty black-and-white and without a word of dialogue, this frantic flick finishes in a speedy 55 minutes. Considered a fixture of cyberpunk cinema, though fans of the Tetsuo pics will find this easier to follow. D: Ishii. C: Asano, Masatoshi Nagase, Yoshiki Arizono. SUNCENT CINEMAWORKS/TAKI

END, THE See VIRUS

E.S.P./SPY See ESPY

ESPY (J 1974, US 1975) **½ Groovy, man. In ESPY, an action thriller featuring spies with paranormal powers, we find that even the world of espionage is hip to the fashion sense of the times. It's the heady days of the mid-1970s, with our main female operative favoring hip-hugging pantsuits and her male cohorts sporting thick heads of helmet hair. These kooky cats also possess an amazing array of mental abilities: telekinesis, telepathy, teleportation, tele-everything it seems. They'll need the whole shebang to combat an evil outfit with similar psychic skills who are assassinating global bigwigs. It's all derived from a novel by Sakyo Komatsu, who also wrote "Japan Sinks" and "Sayonara Jupiter." Not to blow the ending, but when all is said and done, we learn that "love is the driving force behind ESP." I'm down with it. AKA: E.S.P./SPY. D: Jun Fukuda. C: Hiroshi Fujioka, Kaoru Yumi, Masao Kusakani. TOHO

EVIL BRAIN FROM OUTER SPACE (J 1959, US 1964) *½ Last, but not least, of the four Starman movies, and undoubtedly the darkest. The Japanese "Man of Steel" is at the ready when an assortment of aberrant creatures are unleashed on Earth by a soggy alien brain. We're subjected to the likes of fanged mutants with misty radioactive breath, witchy women, and martial arts assailants garbed in Batman gear. Wearing his trusty globe meter wristwatch (which enables the user to fly, detect radiation, and understand all dialects) our hero Starman is always in the right place at the right time, saving the hides of precocious kids and helpless adults alike. The pace is fast and furious; it's not a stretch to surmise that the Starman films were an inspiration for ULTRAMAN and the numerous other superhero TV shows that would later be all the rage in Japan. This flick, however, is brought to you in basic black-and-white. D: Teruo Ishii, Akira Mitsuwa, Koreyoshi Akasaka. C: Ken Utsui, Junko Ikeuchi. FUJI/SHINTOHO

F

FRANKENSTEIN CONQUERS THE WORLD (J 1965, US 1966) *** Toho's "big" attempt to go Universal. The pulsating heart of the Frankenstein monster, perfectly preserved in liquid protein, is shipped from Nazi Germany to Hiroshima at the close of World War II. Said to be indestructible, the uber organ survives the devastating effects of the A-bomb. Some 20 years later, a feral teen resembling ol' Frankie is spotted roaming the area in search of dogs, rabbits, and who knows what else to devour. Somehow, the ravenous lad has emerged with the nuked ticker, and he's growing at an abnormal rate. To complicate the situation, along comes an 80-foot-tall leaping lizard known as Baragon. This paunchy, floppy-eared mischief-maker spits lightning, and burrows underground with ease. His diverse diet includes pigs, horses, and chickens. (He gleefully burps up feathers after one satisfying feeding.) No, this is not a film for animal lovers. Baragon also scarfs down a bunch of unlucky humans – and Frankie boy gets the blame. It's but a matter of time before the two ultimately tangle in the slam-bang finale. Nick Adams, in an earnest performance as a compassionate doctor, tries to figure it all out. A tussle with a flimsy giant octopus was edited out of the American version. D: Ishiro Honda. C: Adams, Kumi Mizuno, Tadao Takashima. TOHO

FUJITIVE ALIEN (J 1978, US 1986) *½ Watch solely for the camp appeal. Culled from episodes of a Japanese TV series, this screwy space saga certainly hums along at a vigorous pace. But we're definitely talking budget-challenged here. A conscientious alien named "Ken" (played by Tatsuya Azuma) is branded a traitor by his own kind for refusing to kill humans. He takes refuge with the earthling crew of the Bacchus-3, a sturdy spacecraft helmed by the boozy Captain Joe (Jo Shishido). A Star Wars-inspired chase ensues, with Ken's former buddies – the feared Wolf Raiders – in hot pursuit. Can't we all just get along? Best to catch the MYSTERY SCIENCE THEATER 3000 razzing, if you can. STAR FORCE: FUJITIVE ALIEN II would follow. D: Minoru Kanaya, Kiyosumi Kuzakawa. C: Azuma, Shishido, Miyuki Tanigawa, Choei Takahashi. TSUBURAYA PRODUCTIONS

G

GAMERA: ATTACK OF LEGION (J 1996, US 2003) *** The second of director Shusuke Kaneko's highly-praised Gamera trilogy has the large-and-in-charge turtle defending Earth from thousands of crablike creepers from outer space. Bright young researcher Midori Honami (Miki Mizuno) is summoned from the Sapporo Science Center, but the mysterious life form – known as Legion – is stone-cold vicious. Things get really weird when one of the hostile critters suddenly grows to immense heights. The supersized Legion wounds a weary Gamera with one of its pointy appendages and the green blood gushes freely. Military forces quickly arrive, and – as often is the case in daikaiju films – bombard the wrong monster. Man, that's aggravating. Shinji Higuchi's special effects exertions frequently push the limits; the guy has a healthy zeal for explosions! Gamera's schoolgirl pal Asagi Kusanagi (Ayako

Fujitani) returns to offer spiritual support. D: Kaneko. C: Toshiyuki Nagashima, Mizuno, Tamotsu Ishibashi, Mitsuru Fukioshi, Yusuke Kawazu. DAIEI

GAMERA: GUARDIAN OF THE UNIVERSE (J 1995, US 1997) **** Wow! Gamera, the beloved giant turtle who jet-thrusted his way into the hearts of television viewers in the 1970s, triumphantly reemerges in this enthusiastic, inventive effort that ranks among the all-time greatest daikaiju pics. Unlike the Showa Era series, the new Gamera movies are decidedly serious affairs. The toothy terrapin is stirred from a deep sleep to take on a trio of Gyaos, the flat-headed, human-munchin', sonic-beam shootin' birdies first seen in RETURN OF THE GIANT MONSTERS. He's aided by a teenage girl (played by actor Steven Seagal's daughter, Ayako Fujitani) who is psychically linked to the big reptile through a mystical, comma-shaped amulet. There are several standout moments. (You'll hold your breath when a determined Gyaos dive-bombs straight toward the occupied dugout of the Fukuoka Dome.) Gamera now has the ability to regurgitate blistering balls o' fire – a particularly effective attack. Shinji Higuchi received the Japanese equivalent of the Academy Award for his astonishing special effects work, and director Shusuke Kaneko rightfully earned rave reviews. Kaneko, Higuchi, and screenwriter Kazumori Ito would also join forces for the splendid sequels: GAMERA: ATTACK OF LEGION and GAMERA: REVENGE OF IRIS. D: Kaneko. C: Tsuyoshi Ihara, Akira Onodera, Fujitani, Shinobu Nakayama, Yukijiro Hotaru. DAIEI

GAMERA: REVENGE OF IRIS (J 1999, 2003) ***½ The vivacious Heisei Era of Gamera films concludes in fine style as the huge turtle protects our planet from an odd, cephalopodic monstrosity with tubular tentacles. Ayana, a bitter kid who mistakenly blames Gamera for her parents' deaths four years earlier, discovers the newly-hatched nemesis in the cave of an ancient shrine; she raises the lil' one, vengeance foremost on her mind. The rotten rapscallion surprisingly offs everyone in Ayana's rustic little village, and rapidly enlarges. Meanwhile, Gamera's arch enemy, the dreaded Gyaos, have returned. The sturdy-shelled reptile blows apart two of the bat-like birdies with efficient fireball breath-blasts, but sets the Shibuya District of Tokyo ablaze. We've come to expect the unexpected from special effects maestro Shinji Higuchi; the ground-level view of the combustible cityscape, with bodies catapulting through the air, is unlike anything ever depicted in a Japanese sci-fi feature. Back from GAMERA: GUARDIAN OF THE UNIVERSE is ornithologist Mayumi Nagamine (Shinobu Nakayama), who teams up with a couple of former associates – the harried Inspector Osaka (Yukijiro Hotaru) and telepathic teen Asagi Kusanagi (Ayako Fujitano) – to provide the human drama. Gamera would eventually reappear in 2006's GAMERA THE BRAVE. D: Shusuke Kaneko. C: Nakayama, Ai Maeda, Fujitani. DAIEI

GAMERA: SUPER MONSTER (J 1980, US 1980) ** Gamera, the enormous twirling turtle with the dull-white tusks, surprisingly resurfaced after a nine-year hiatus as a restructured Daiei Studios was back in business after going bankrupt in the early 1970s. Essentially, this is an unofficial retrospective of Gamera's cinematic career, as over one-third of the film is stock footage of the raucous reptile's epic battles with rival monsters Gyaos, Zigra, Viras, Jiger,

Guiron, and Barugon. Alien baddies recruit the notorious creatures to front a calculated takeover of Earth. Fortunately, a trio of high-soaring spacewomen in matching leotards (and the capability to shrink!) are around to assist an overextended Gamera. Of course, this wouldn't be a Gamera movie without a screechy child on hand to torture the viewer; Keichi, a lad who's loopy about turtles, readily performs a whimsical ode to "the children's friend" on electric organ. Fans of the series may bemoan the inclusion of kaiju scuffles already used umpteen times, but the excerpts selected are definitely the cream of the crop. Alas, a noteworthy new scene: Gamera's initial appearance in the pic, a cool shot of the recognizable cooter sneaking a peek from behind the the tallest of city buildings. AKA: SPACE MONSTER GAMERA, SUPER MONSTER. D: Noriaki Yuasa. C: Mach Fumiake, Yaeko Kojimi. DAIEI

GAMERA THE BRAVE (J 2006, US 2006) ***½ Gamera is back (!) in a heartfelt family flick that nestles itself comfortably amidst the sizable turtle's kid-friendly Showa Era roots and the darker, critically-acclaimed trilogy of the 1990s. Toru, a young boy reeling from his mother's recent passing, finds a small egg in a settlement of rocks; it cracks open and a tiny baby turtle wriggles out. Toru refers to his newbie companion as "Toto," a nickname his mother had lovingly bestowed upon him. Toto is soon flying and puffing mini-fireballs, and it's apparent that the rascally reptile, getting bigger by the day, is a Gamera offspring. Not what Toru had in mind, but good timing for Japan. Zedus, a freakishly large iguana with a long, piercing tongue and a thirst for human blood, has appeared on the mainland. The fledgling Gamera, bless his heart, ain't afraid of no overgrown lizard. One of the first productions from Kadokawa after purchasing Daiei, the film didn't meet box-office expectations, putting future Gamera projects on hold. Regardless, it's a charming little picture that will surely appeal to the moppets. D: Ryuto Tasaki. C: Ryo Tomioka, Kaho, Kanji Tsuda. KADOKAWA

GAMERA THE INVINCIBLE (J 1965, US 1966) ** A nuclear bomb blast unearths a monstrous, fire-breathing turtle from the Arctic's icy depths. And guess what? The dang thing can fly! That's right, fly. Sometimes, even, like a jet-propelled discus. The raging reptile instinctively proceeds to Tokyo to wreak the usual havoc. Run away, extras! Run away! Daiei's attempt to capitalize on Toho's hugely popular Godzilla franchise, this unpretentious offering (shot in plain ol' black-and-white) spawned a series of increasingly quirkier, decisively kiddie-geared sequels. Fittingly enough, we're introduced here to a recurring theme in later Gamera flicks. Beneath that hard shell is a soft spot for children, even the annoying ones. The turtle-crazy boy in this tale is graciously helped out of a tough jam by his ginormous, newfound friend. The backroom banter of veteran actors Albert Dekker and Brian Donlevy is prominent in the American release. The original version (**½) has shown up in recent years, also dubbed in English. (The MYSTERY SCIENCE THEATER 3000 send-up is a hoot.) AKA: GAMMERA THE INVINCIBLE. D: Noriaki Yuasa. C: Donlevy, Dekker, Eiji Funikoshi, Harumi Kiritachi. DAIEI

GAMERA VS. BARUGON See WAR OF THE MONSTERS

GAMERA VS. GAOS See RETURN OF THE GIANT MONSTERS

GAMERA VS. GYAOS See RETURN OF THE GIANT MONSTERS

GAMERA VS. GUIRON See ATTACK OF THE MONSTERS

GAMERA VS. JIGER See GAMERA VS. MONSTER X

GAMERA VS. MONSTER X (J 1970, US 1970) *** Gamera is . . . *knocked up*? Well, not really, but our favorite oversized turtle suffers a nasty case of nausea here in his sixth high-flying film adventure. A sacred stone statue (slated for showcase at Expo '70 in Osaka) is removed from a South Pacific island, releasing a spear-shooting triceratops with a quick temper named Jiger. Arguably the fiercest of Gamera's Showa Era adversaries, the relentless Jiger is a kaiju of many talents: leaping, levitating, suctioning, et al. And just when you think you've seen it all, Jiger utilizes a retractable tail stinger to inject its gunky larva inside an unsuspecting Gamera. The sickly terrapin collapses in a nearby bay, turning a chalky white. But don't fear. Our child protagonists, Hiroshi and Tommy, have a mini-submarine . . . and a plan. Featuring imaginative monster skirmishes, the use of stock footage (prevalent in DESTROY ALL PLANETS and ATTACK OF THE MONSTERS) is limited to the opening credits. AKA: GAMERA VS. JIGER. D: Noriaki Yuasa. C: Tsutomu Takakuwa, Kelly Varis, Kathleen Murphy, Kon Omura. DAIEI

GAMERA VS. VIRAS See DESTROY ALL PLANETS

GAMERA VS. ZIGRA (J 1971, US 1987) **½ Daiei's last film before collapsing into bankruptcy finds our pal Gamera, the giant flying turtle, with bloodshot eyes, yellowing teeth, and (I'm guessing) serious halitosis. The hygiene just isn't there. And the lethargy! The big guy's not even "saucer spinning" while airborne. He needs to pull it together – and fast. Zigra, an obnoxious deep sea shark from outer space, is keen on Earth's boundless oceans and fancies the meaty taste of human beings. Gamera intercedes but is promptly knocked out cold by the squidgy Zigra's wacky paralyzing ray. Oh well, he could definitely use the shut eye. Meanwhile, to show he means business, Zigra dispatches an intergalactic girlie in black go-go boots to chase a couple of harmless kids around a Japanese marine park. Maybe it's the children. Maybe it's the sleep. Maybe it's the groovy surf sounds of Shinsuke Kikuchi's music score. But an invigorated Gamera awakens to firmly settle matters, adding the final touches with a riveting marimba solo on his foe's pliant back fins. Gotta hand it to the turtle. He's bad, he's bad, he's bad. D: Noriaki Yuasa. C: Eiko Yanami, Reiko Kasahara, Koji Fujiyama. DAIEI

GAMMERA THE INVINCIBLE See GAMERA THE INVINCIBLE

GANTZ (J 2010, US 2011) ** Those who prefer the tight, quick editing of Hollywood action fare may find GANTZ, with its lengthy character intros, hard to get next to. The flick does, however, fall into a steady rhythm. Two teen dudes, played by J-pop star Kazunari Ninomiya and L:

CHANGE THE WORLD's Kenichi Matsuyama, rescue a drunkard from the subway tracks but, unfortunately, get smushed by a train. They rematerialize in a room with a strange black orb that coerces them – and other recently-deceased folks – to snuff out aliens hiding on Earth. The ETs are a curious sort: onion-loving creatures, a boombox-toting robot, an ill-mannered Majin look-alike, and a multi-armed, slicin'-and-dicin' menace. There's also a humongous, mean-spirited Buddha running rampant. Our participants, attired in black leather and furnished with superhuman skills, are rewarded points for offing the interstellar dwellers. When 100 points are accumulated, the recipient can choose to either return from the dead or revive a slain comrade. The exciting fight sequences, with Makoto Kamiya's excellent CGI effects in the forefront, give the pic a shot in the arm. Followed by a sequel, GANTZ: PERFECT ANSWER. D: Shinsuke Sato. C: Ninomiya, Matsuyama, Yuriko Yoshitaka, Kanata Hingo, Natsuna, Tomorowo Taguchi. GANTZ FILM PARTNERS

GANTZ: PERFECT ANSWER (J 2010, US 2011) **½ Ahh . . . the element of mystery. A lot of the shenanigans in this follow-up to GANTZ transpire amid the murky din of nightfall. Faces come and go but you'd need some sort of cinematic night goggles to figure out who's who. That said, there's a brief preamble that conveniently brings the viewer up to speed. An enigmatic black sphere – Gantz – continues to resurrect the dearly departed to pursue and kill otherworldly types residing on Earth. This time, the extraterrestrials – mighty perturbed at being hunted down – have assumed the identities of actual human folk. Bullets fly and swords slash as a tumultuous confrontation on a subway train leads to 84 casualties. A dogged detective, investigating numerous reported sightings of dead people now very much alive, tries to piece it all together. Japanese teen idols Kazunari Ninomiya and Kenichi Matsuyama resume their roles as best buds governed by Gantz's puzzling grip. Based on an ongoing anime series and manga created by Hiroya Oku. AKA: GANTZ 2: PEFECT ANSWER. D: Shinsuke Sato. C: Ninomiya, Matsuyama, Yuriko Yoshitaka, Kanata Hongo, Go Ayano, Ayumi Ito, Tomorowo Taguchi. GANTZ FILM PARTNERS

GANTZ 2: PERFECT ANSWER See GANTZ: PERFECT ANSWER

GAPPA, THE TRIPHIBIAN MONSTER See MONSTER FROM A PREHISTORIC PLANET

GEHARA, THE LONG-HAIRED GIANT MONSTER (J 2009, US 2009) **½ An amusing spoof of daikaiju flicks, GEHARA is a 20-minute made-for-TV movie that was screened at a number of Asian film fests in the States. A peculiar creature with greasy, stringy black hair rises from the sea to cause a stir in Japan. When the gassy gargantuan lets loose with a wicked fart, Japan Self-Defense Forces troops are left weak and woozy by the vile fumes. Will the military's vaunted "gas vortical device" save the day? Comedian Jan Muira developed the clever script, and Shinji Higuchi (the Gamera Heisei Era trilogy) supervised the extraordinary special effects. The Japanese DVD release includes 80 minutes of bonus footage. D: Kiyotaka Taguchi. C: Ken Osawa, Mina Fujii, Shiro Sano, Jiji Bu, Mina Fujii,

Tomorowo Taguchi. NHK (JAPANESE BROADCASTING CORPORATION)

GENOCIDE (J 1968, US 1969) ** Break out the insect repellant. New-and-improved breeds of killer bugs are buzzing about! Seldom seen in the U.S. and rather hard to locate, GENOCIDE is director Kazui Nihonmatsu's next film after the wonderfully daft THE X FROM OUTER SPACE. This one, though, is played closer to the vest. A plane flies smack-dab into a swarm of bees, crash-lands on a Japanese island, and loses the H-bomb they were lugging around. As American military heads and Russian spies compete to find the missing explosive, an obsessed scientist (Kathy Horan) readies her army of deadly arthropods to destroy the world. A concentration camp survivor, she's determined to bring a halt to mankind's cruel tendencies. And these are some unpleasant pests. Pass on this flick if you're allergic to bee stings. AKA: WAR OF THE INSECTS. D: Nihonmatsu. C: Keisuke Sonoi, Yusuke Kawazu, Emi Shindo, Horan, Chico Roland. SHOCHIKU

GHIDORAH, THE THREE-HEADED MONSTER (J 1964, US 1965) *** A massive meteor hits with a thud in a mountainous region of Japan and our title character – a hyperkinetic, tri-headed space dragon with a penchant for disgorging devastating lightning bolts – dramatically emerges. A princess-turned-psychic alien (Bond girl Akiko Wakabayashi) warns the skeptical locals of impending disaster. They yuck it up heartily until Godzilla and Rodan (in the beaked one's first outing since its 1956 debut) suddenly appear. Any notion of the two gettin' chummy is quickly dispelled as the gigantic flying reptile pokes

Godzilla's pate like a demented woodpecker. The monster brawls are intentionally played for laughs. Godzilla even suffers the indignity of having his privates singed by one of Ghidorah's searing electrical discharges. Yep, you got it: crotch humor, Toho-style. Mothra (in larva form) is also around for more sticky fun. The frenzied finale, with Earth's monsters defending their turf against an irascible Ghidorah, is pure unabashed slapstick. AKA: GHIDRAH, THE THREE-HEADED MONSTER. D: Ishiro Honda. C: Yosuke Natsuki, Yuriko Hoshi, Hiroshi Koizumi, the Peanuts (Emi and Yumi Ito). TOHO

GHIDRAH, THE THREE-HEADED MONSTER See GHIDORAH, THE THREE-HEADED MONSTER

G.I. SAMURAI See TIME SLIP

GIGANTIS, THE FIRE MONSTER See GODZILLA RAIDS AGAIN

GODZILLA 1985 (J 1984, US 1985) ** The big lizard's first film in nine years is a direct sequel to the original GOJIRA/GODZILLA, KING OF THE MONSTERS. That's difficult to wrap one's brain around, since it ignores all other Godzilla movies as if they didn't exist. Even so, it's a decent enough story, and the special effects from Teruyoshi Nakano are terrific. There's an amazing scene where a voracious Godzilla consumes a considerable amount of radiation from a nuclear power plant, his jagged dorsal fins brightly pulsating. Never before has the righteous reptile's atomic breath illumed with such vibrance. This is serious-minded stuff; noticeably absent is the quirkiness of Toho's kaiju eiga of the 1960s and 1970s. Raymond Burr even reprises his role as the solemn newspaperman he portrayed in the very first G pic. D: Koji Hashimoto, R.J. Kizer. C: Burr, Ken Tanaka, Yasuko Sawaguchi, Yosuke Natsuki, Keibu Kobayashi. TOHO

GODZILLA 2000 (J 1999, US 2000) *** Is that a giant, fossilized turd gliding sky-high toward Tokyo? Naw, it's actually a sleek, silvery flying saucer in disguise – with designs on cloning our favorite hot-breathed behemoth! Things go awry, as they often do, and a clawed, scraggly creature with poor posture is spawned. Meet Orga, certainly one of Godzilla's most disturbing foes, ever. Coming but two years after the anticlimactic TriStar GODZILLA, this one's a welcome relief for dedicated followers of the large lizard. Toho restakes its claim to the big guy in grand fashion. Godzilla's fiery radioactive stream is on overdrive, flashing an intense, vivid white. Wait 'til you catch the weird and wild finish, where Orga swallows a bit more than it can chew! The last Japanese-made Godzilla film to date to receive a major theatrical run in America; nonetheless, the Millenium Era of G flicks kicks off with renewed vigor. D: Takao Okawara. C: Takehiro Murata, Naomi Nashida, Hiroshi Abe, Mayu Suzuki, Shiro Sano. TOHO

GODZILLA AGAINST MECHAGODZILLA (J 2002, US 2004) ***½ Mechagodzilla, the titanic robot semblance of Godzilla, returns in all its gleaming glory – but with a twist. This time around, the Japanese government constructs a souped-up version of the metallurgic marvel *integrating the skeleton of the original Godzilla that perished in 1954!* Besides the standard assortment of lasers, masers, and missiles, Mecha G (also referred to as Kiryu in this pic) is tricked out with an "absolute zero cannon" – a weapon which can freeze-blast *anything* to smithereens! Godzilla is his usual ornery self; the opening sequence – in particular – packs a powerful punch, as the monstrous mutated lizard mixes it up with Japan Self-Defense Forces in a torrential downpour. Ten soldiers are killed, and young pilot Akane Yashiro (Yumiko Shaku) shoulders the responsibility. A dour Akane does a lot of soul searching while awaiting her chance at redemption. She's also constantly hit on by a jittery Kiryu Project scientist. Well, you can't blame a guy for trying. Baseball slugger Hideki "Godzilla" Matsui is featured in a cameo role. D: Masaaki Tezuka. C: Shaku, Shin Takuma, Kana Onodera. TOHO

GODZILLA AND MOTHRA: THE BATTLE FOR EARTH (J 1992, US 1998) *** One thing for sure we've learned about an often grumpy Godzilla over the years – he unequivocally hates bugs. Be it spider, praying mantis, dragonfly, or moth, the roarin' reptile has no need for 'em. Out to pester him this time is the resplendent airborne insect Mothra and her black-winged cousin Battra, a former protector of Earth gone astray. This fun-filled flick is greatly influenced by the Showa Era classics MOTHRA (1961) and GODZILLA VS. THE THING (1964), as our favorite singing twin fairies (now dubbed "the Cosmos") are on hand to look after Mothra's giant egg and admonish humankind for its destruction of our planet. Mothra and Battra (a mighty impressive monster, by the way) morph from caterpillar larvae into graceful adult wing-flutterers; tokusatsu enthusiasts will truly enjoy their colorful encounter in the night skies of Yokohama. A feisty Godzilla joins the fray on ground level, and it's simply one of the best daikaiju tussles ever realized on film. Where else you gonna see one of the world's tallest Ferris wheels put to use as a weapon? Koichi Kawakita continues to astound, as he brings Japanese special effects into the modern age. D: Takao Okawara. C: Tetsuya Bessho, Satomi Kobayashi, Takehiko Murata, Makoto Otake. TOHO

GODZILLA: FINAL WARS (J 2004, US 2005) **** Say what you will about FINAL WARS but it definitely elicits a strong reaction. The jury is split on director Ryuhei Kitamura's radical take on the legendary lizard's legacy but the pic brazenly captures the "anything goes" mindset that drew many of us to the magic of kaijudom as youngsters. And those who appreciate Kitamura's exhilarating style of moviemaking (atypical camera angles, creative editing, full-blown special effects, and dynamic fight scenes) won't be disappointed. The action-packed plot is respectfully borrowed from DESTROY ALL MONSTERS, as alien evildoers unloose Earth's giant monsters to obliterate the world. Not only do we see essential figures Mothra, Rodan, and King Ghidorah; we're also treated to rare appearances by the likes of mouthwatering lobster Ebirah, lion-god King Caesar (nee Seesar), sea snake Manda, and the gloppy Hedorah ("the Smog Monster"). Godzilla is freed from his icy confinement in the South Pole to save the planet. Gotengo, the shimmery-smooth flying sub from ATRAGON, does the honors; its crew is led by the gruff Captain Gordon, played with gusto by the thick-mustachioed Don Frye. Fearlessly supporting the cause is the Earth Defense Force, an elite combat unit featuring mutant humans with fantastic fightin' abilities. Undaunted, the maniacal alien leader (a gung-ho performance from Kazuki Kitamura) keeps the creatures a-comin': there's resilient armadillo Anguirus (dig that rolling ball attack!), agile cyborg Gigan, pesky bugs Kamakuras and Kumonga, and a problematic new foe for the Big G, the Predator-inspired Monster X. Godzilla also contends with his American counterpart, Zilla, in a segment sure to delight diehard G fans. Minilla (a.k.a. Minya, Godzilla's pudgeball son) also tags along. Promoted as Godzilla's 50th anniversary film, popular Showa Era actors Kumi Mizuno, Kenji Sahara, and Akira Takarada are cast in prominent roles. Keith Emerson of influential prog-rockers Emerson, Lake, and Palmer contributed to the synth-heavy soundtrack. D: R. Kitamura. C: Masahiro Matsuoka, Rei Kikukawa, Frye, K. Kitamura, Maki Mizuno, Kane Kosugi, Masakatsu Funaki. TOHO

GODZILLA, KING OF THE MONSTERS (J 1954, US 1956) *** The one that started it all. An H-bomb test rouses an enormous, fire-breathing saurian from a deep slumber – and he's mighty ticked. Tokyo is leveled, and the rest of Japan is next. Filmed in black-and-white, the realistic depiction of a metropolis laid to waste is eerily similar to documentary footage of Hiroshima and Nagasaki shot just a decade earlier. Originally released in Japan as GOJIRA in 1954, scenes with Raymond Burr as an attentive news correspondent were added for the U.S. version. The Japanese archetype (****) is deemed by purists as the superior film and has a cogent anti-nuclear message only hinted at in the American reworking. Toho's celebrated trio of director Ishiro Honda, special effects supervisor Eiji Tsuburaya, and music composer Akira Ifukube created the template for a new, unique genre with their work in this cinematic benchmark. The indefatigable Haruo Nakajima would also make a name for himself as the foremost suit actor of his generation, sweating it out in Godzilla's rubber outerwear – often under challenging circumstances – for the next 18 years. AKA: GOJIRA. D: Honda, Terry Moore. C: Burr, Akira Takarada, Momoko Kochi, Akihiko Hirata, Takashi Shimura. TOHO

GODZILLA, MOTHRA, AND KING GHIDORAH: GIANT MONSTERS ALL-OUT ATTACK (J 2001, US 2004) ***½ An interesting aspect of the Millenium Era of Godzilla movies is the series' deliberate disregard for continuity. There's nothing in the script, for instance, linking this film with its predecessor, GODZILLA VS. MEGAGUIRUS. The open-minded approach has allowed directors the freedom to generate some of the more daring and distinctive G pics of any period. Shusuke Kaneko, who helmed the inventive Gamera trilogy of the 1990s, gets his shot here and he's not afraid to defy convention. A milky-eyed Godzilla (he literally has no pupils) is on the rampage, a living embodiment of the tormented, forgotten souls of Japanese soldiers who perished in the Pacific War. A mysterious old man (Eisei Amamoto, in what would be his final big-screen part) asserts that a trio of creatures that protected Japan in ancient times will arise to fight the omnipotent reptile. Sure enough, the "guardian monsters" soon appear: the bounding dino-dog, Baragon; a smaller-than-usual representation of Mothra (doing the whole "larva-to-moth" thing); and a stubby-legged King Ghidorah (in an unfamiliar "good guy" role for the triple-headed dragon). A well-developed subplot focuses on the relationship between a persistent TV news reporter

(Chiharu Niiyama) and her Navy commander father (Ryudo Uzaki). They both pursue Godzilla: she for a sensational story, and he out of a sense of duty. Incidentally, those old scallywags Anguirus and Varan were Kaneko's original choices to join Baragon as guardian monsters but Toho insisted on the higher-profile daikaiju. D: Kaneko. C: Niiyama, Uzaki, Masahiro Kobayashi, Shiro Sano. TOHO

GODZILLA ON MONSTER ISLAND See GODZILLA VS. GIGAN

GODZILLA RAIDS AGAIN (J 1955, US 1959) ** You can't keep a good monster down. Eight months after being dissolved to nothingness by the dreaded oxygen destroyer, Godzilla was back for this rather somber sequel. The atom-age menace (he's really, we're told, another of the species) is discovered grappling with Anguirus, a tenacious ankylosaur, on an uninhabited Japanese isle. The terrible twosome tumble off a cliff into the water below, but eventually resurface to trample Osaka. The kaiju clashes are unusually fast and ferocious; a special effects camera was set incorrectly for the shoot but Eiji Tsuburaya, tokusatsu main man, liked the results. Oddly, this film was released in the US in 1959 as GIGANTIS, THE FIRE MONSTER to give moviegoers the impression this was a new monster – and not a reissue of GODZILLA, KING OF THE MONSTERS. Lensed in black-and-white like its precursor but without the obvious anti-nuke bent. Keye Luke (of KUNG FU fame) provides the spoon-fed narration. AKA: GIGANTIS, THE FIRE MONSTER. D: Motoyoshi Oda. C: Hiroshi Koizumi, Setsuko Wakayama, Mindru Chiaki. TOHO

GODZILLA: RESURGENCE See SHIN GODZILLA

GODZILLA: TOKYO S.O.S. (J 2003, US 2004) ***½ The only sequel in the Millenium Series of Godzilla films, TOKYO S.O.S. follows in the wake of the superb GODZILLA AGAINST MECHAGODZILLA – and doesn't disappoint. A lean and mean Godzilla drops by just as the final spit and polish is applied to the redoubtable reptile's metallic equivalent, Mechagodzilla. The prodigious robot, designed to defend Japan, utilizes the skeletal framework of the original Godzilla – which doesn't sit well with a couple of plucky gals from Infant Island. Yep, it's Mothra's teensy-weensy twin fairies, now called the Shobijin, who warn that Godzilla's bones must be returned to their resting place in the sea or all hell will break loose. The Japanese government is less than receptive, prompting the mammoth moth's arrival on the mainland. Concurrently, things are shakin' on the Shobijin's home turf, as a pair of caterpillars hatch from a massive egg and swim to Tokyo to help out mother. The flick borrows at will from Mothra's early Showa Era movies, and that's not a bad thing. Masaaki Tekuza, director of both this picture and its forerunner, unites an efficient storyline with expeditious action and eye-catching visual effects. Mechagodzilla, with its high-powered masers, missiles, and other gadgetry, inflicts a big-time hurtin' on Godzilla. The Sony/TriStar home release includes a cool behind-the-scenes look at Eiichi Asada's special effects squad working the wires. A side note: Kamoebas, the huge turtle from YOG, MONSTER FROM SPACE, makes a brief appearance, albeit as a corpse. D: Tezuka. C: Noboru Kaneko, Miho Yoshioka, Mitsuki Koga, Hiroshi Koizumi. TOHO

GODZILLA VS. BIOLLANTE (J 1989, US 1992) **½ The definitive Godzilla flick for botanists. The Lizard King gets tangled in the tendrils of a genetically-engineered plant monstrosity created by the brilliant Dr. Shiragami, an unorthodox scientific researcher with a green thumb. A beefed-up Godzilla (now sporting bodybuilder pecs) endures bacteria missiles piercing his skin, a caustic substance spat in his face by his title adversary, and a barrage of projectiles from the Super X-2 (a spiffed-up version of the airborne combat conveyance damaged in this movie's prequel, GODZILLA 1985). Now remote-controlled, the X-2 also features a "fire mirror" that reflects Godzilla's radioactive breath right back at him with 1,000 times the oomph. Oh, and we're also introduced to psychic Miki Saegusa, played by Megumi Odaka. Miki would remain a fixture in the G pictures of the Heisei Era (1984-1995). Fans had to patiently wait until 2012 for this film's official DVD release stateside. D: Kazuki Omori. C: Kunihiko Mitamura, Yoshiko Tanaka, Masanobu Takashima, Koji Takahashi, Odaka. TOHO

GODZILLA VS. DESTOROYAH (J 1995, US 1999) ***½ Something is horribly amiss with the almighty Godzilla. Lava-colored splotches scorch the fabled lizard's hardened hide as he furiously lays waste to Hong Kong. With his nuclear fission rate rising to an unthinkable level, Godzilla will soon explode – and vaporize the entire freakin' planet. Actually, it was heavily publicized by Toho prior to this pic's release that the revered reptile would not make it out alive. Still, it's tough to watch him slowly die; the colossal creature is clearly in some serious pain. Plus, he's dealing with 10-foot-tall creepy-crawlers (the "Destoroyah") originating from the area in which the devastating oxygen destroyer was used to dissipate the very first Godzilla in 1954. The Japanese military temporarily puts the freeze on the big guy with anti-nuclear cold weaponry; he thaws, but is then in meltdown mode! Eventually, the multitude of Destoroyah merge to form a horrendous, flying nightmare. Godzilla Jr. (Little Godzilla from GODZILLA VS. SPACE GODZILLA, now mutated) is present for the emotion-drenched ending, which is alternately sad, shocking, and touching. This would also be the last Godzilla film for longtime producer, Tomoyuki Tanaka. Tanaka, who primarily envisioned the conception of Godzilla, would pass away in 1997. AKA: GODZILLA VS. DESTROYER. D: Takao Okawara. C: Takuro Tatsumi, Yoko Ishino, Yasufumi Hayashi, Megumi Odaka. TOHO

GODZILLA VS. DESTROYER See GODZILLA VS. DESTOROYAH

GODZILLA VS. GIGAN (J 1972, US 1977) **½ Call the exterminators! Alien cockroaches (in human guise) have set out to subjugate Earth, recruiting the tri-headed King Ghidorah and bird-like buddy Gigan to do their dirty work. Godzilla, laying low on Monster Island, is coaxed out of retirement by his prickly friend Angilas (a.k.a Anguirus) to defend the planet. The former enemies are now, literally, on speaking terms as they blurt out sentence fragments in distorted English to each other. Yep, this is one wacked-out flick. Frankly, with the exception of the hyperactive Gigan, the kaiju appear mighty sluggish. The gangly-necked Ghidorah looks flat-out sedated. A subdued Godzilla can barely muster up enough energy to employ his powerful atomic breath. Perhaps the repetitive jabs to the head from the cocksure Gigan's metallic talons have rendered him groggy. And check this out: That's a frickin' *buzzsaw* protruding from Gigan's belly. Ouch-a-rama! AKA: GODZILLA ON MONSTER ISLAND. D: Jun Fukuda. C: Hiroshi Ichikawa, Yuriko Hishimi, Minoru Takashima, Tomoko Umeda. TOHO

GODZILLA VS. HEDORAH See GODZILLA VS. THE SMOG MONSTER

GODZILLA VS. KING GHIDORAH (J 1991, US 1998) ***1/2 Much appreciated by daikaiju fans and critics alike. Time travelers from the 23rd century turn up in modern-day Japan to warn of its upcoming annihilation by Godzilla. It's a bunch of hogwash, of course. Dismayed by Nippon's eventual emergence as a dominant economic power, the dirty double-crossers summon forth King Ghidorah, the monstrous three-headed dragon, to demolish the country. Meanwhile, a bigger and badder Godzilla rises from the ocean's depths. His potent nuclear breath on full throttle, the giant therapod effortlessly blasts apart one of King G's heads! The battle royale at picture's end (with an ill-humored Godzilla squaring off against a mechanically-enhanced Ghidorah) is a dazzling display of Koichi Kawakita's special effects prowess. Kawakita, in fact, won the Japanese version of the Academy Award for his work in this film. Director Kazuki Omori has evident admiration for THE TERMINATOR, incorporating time-trekking themes and featuring a stoic android (played with steely perfection by Robert Scott Field) as one of the able cast's more memorable characters. D: Omori. C: Kosuke Toyohara,

Anna Nakagawa, Megumi Odaka, Katsuhiko Sasaki, Akiji Kobayashi. TOHO

GODZILLA VS. MECHAGODZILLA (J 1974, US 1977) ** Gotta admit it's pretty darn clever that Toho created a giant robot replica of the venerable King of the Monsters. Seemingly invincible, the mighty, silver-hued mecha is equipped with finger missiles, eye and chest lasers, and flight capabilities. Godzilla struggles mightily with the titanium wonder until a convenient lightning storm increases the big fella's strength. Made during the ultra-campy era of G flicks, which helps explain why an evil group of apes from outer space (yep, you read it right) are attempting the obligatory world takeover. And, hold on, it's a newcomer. Okinawan legend King Seesar, a shaggy-haired, hard-charging man-beast, is beckoned from his mountain home. Is he more dog or lion – I don't know – but his ears perk up like an alert watchdog when he's excited. Anguirus, the prehistoric armadillo, hangs around long enough to get a broken jaw from on-again, off-again pal, Godzilla. But, alas, appearances can be deceiving. A subplot involving Interpol agents is slipped in for a little intrigue. AKA: GODZILLA VS. THE BIONIC MONSTER, GODZILLA VS. THE COSMIC MONSTER. D: Jun Fukuda. C: Masaaki Daimon, Kazuya Aoyama, Akihiko Hirata, Hiroshi Koizumi, Reiko Tajima. TOHO

GODZILLA VS. MECHAGODZILLA II (J 1993, US 1999) *** For those of you who consider Godzilla as merely a mindless force of destruction, think again. We come to find, in this pleasing Heisei Series entry, that the indomitable dinosaur possesses *two* brains! He'll need all the brainpower he can amass to take on the new-and-improved, silvery smooth Mechagodzilla. The robot doppelganger of the Big G is now friend rather than foe, and is outfitted with an eye-popping arsenal of innovative weapons: plasma grenades, shock anchor cables, paralyzer missiles, etc. And guess who else shows up? Why it's Rodan, in the winged reptile's first major screen stint since the late 1960s. Godzilla, apparently, was gettin' busy since the last time we saw him, as a egg hatches to reveal an adorable baby G. Sure, there's a little mushiness, but serious fans will revel in the pic's enthralling, well-paced monster conflict. Akira Ifukube's intense music score is one of his finest. Of note: Ishiro Honda was brought on to direct but passed away before filming began. D: Takao Okawara. C: Masahiro Takashima, Ryoko Sano, Megumi Odaka. TOHO

GODZILLA VS. MEGAGUIRUS (J 2000, US 2004) **** Just when you think you've beheld every big bug imaginable in the wondrous world of sci-fi cinema, along comes this ingenious flick featuring, of all things, an oversized dragonfly. The creature is spawned when Japanese scientists create a black hole to swallow up, and contain, a surly Godzilla. Interesting idea, but an insect trapped in the hole during the testing phase mutates and then gives birth to a vexatious horde of human-sized dragonflies. Seeking energy, the crazed critters converge upon our favorite giant lizard; the Kaiju King nukes 'em real good but several escape to invigorate the swarm's "chosen one," Megaguirus. The aggressive Megaguirus is surprisingly nimble; a frustrated Godzilla repeatedly misses the mark with his radioactive bad breath. Their final showdown is among the best of any G movie. The Millenium (a.k.a. Shinsei) Series tends to portray the Japan Self-Defense Forces in a positive light. The Anti-Godzilla Command Unit in this pic is led by a brave, young missy (Misato Tanaka) who, at one point, negotiates Godzilla's scaly exterior to implant a high-tech tracking device. Like the film itself, it's a rip-roarin' ride! D: Masaaki Tezuka. C: Tanaka, Shosuke Tanihara, Masato Ibu, Yuriko Hoshi, Toshiyuki Nagashima. TOHO

GODZILLA VS. MEGALON (J 1973, US 1976) **½ Not held in the highest regard by scholarly Godzilla fans, but this is certainly a colorful and fast-paced romp. Mankind's underground nuclear tests threaten to wipe out the legendary underwater kingdom of Seatopia. The Seatopian ruler (Robert Dunham in a toga and white go-go boots) emancipates the multi-talented Megalon, a humongous beetle/cockroach hybrid, to raise a little hell on the surface. Seatopian spies also pilfer a life-sized robot named Jet Jaguar to aid their cause; however, the rocket-powered humanoid dupes his abductors and soars to scenic Monster Island to ask for Godzilla's help. Squashing a nasty, overgrown bug sounds good to the dorsal-finned dino. Jet Jaguar programs itself to enlarge to superhuman size but the Seatopians counter by borrowing the incorrigible galactic bird Gigan from their conspiratorial cronies in the M Space Hunter Nebula. It's a tag-team extravaganza! Godzilla's newfound "flying kick attack" is a jaw-dropper as the bulky lizard appears to magically levitate for a few seconds before knocking down a dumbfounded Gigan. The film's "no holds barred" attitude is similar to the popular Japanese superhero TV shows of the day. D: Jun Fukuda. C: Katsuhiko Sasaki, Hiroyuki Kawase, Yutaka Hayashi,

Kotaro Tomita, Ulf Otsuki, Gentaro Nakajima, Sakyo Mikami. TOHO

GODZILLA VS. MONSTER ZERO (J 1965, US 1970) **** Outrageous monster battles, spectacular special effects, and fantastic outer space action highlight this visual delight from Toho's golden age. Sourpuss aliens from a heretofore undetected planet near Jupiter request our assistance in ridding their world of the triple-headed terror, King Ghidorah. They offer a cure for all diseases (!) in exchange for the services of the one-and-only Godzilla and his pterodactyl colleague, Rodan. Silly humans – you've been tricked! The dirty, stinkin' rats are controlling the monsters, via magnetic waves, with the intention of conquering Earth. It's up to Nick Adams (top-notch as a confident, likeable American astronaut) and a cast of familiar Toho faces to fight the good fight. Godzilla's sixth film, and his behavior is getting downright barmy. One moment he's jabbing like Ali, the next he's dancing a victory jig. Clearly, the studio was beginning to keep younger audiences in mind. AKA: INVASION OF ASTRO-MONSTER, MONSTER ZERO. C: Adams, Akira Takarada, Kumi Mizuno, Akira Kubo, Yoshio Tsuchiya. TOHO

GODZILLA VS. MOTHRA See GODZILLA VS. THE THING

GODZILLA VS. THE BIONIC MONSTER See GODZILLA VS. MECHAGODZILLA

GODZILLA VS. THE COSMIC MONSTER See GODZILLA VS. MECHAGODZILLA

GODZILLA VS. THE SEA MONSTER (J 1966, US 1968) ***½ There's trouble in paradise. Four shipwreck survivors wash up onto the shores of an exotic South Seas Isle and happen upon an evil military operation manufacturing nuclear bombs. Lurking deep within the surrounding waters is a monstrous lobster (the succulent Ebirah) intent on making life miserable for passing boaters. Godzilla, conveniently holed up in one of the island's expansive caverns, is deliberately awakened by the castaways to put an end to the madness. The mighty lizard sizes up his crustaceous foe and promptly tries to boil him alive with a proficient burst of his blazing breath. Heck, the big guy's probably starving. Directed by the versatile Jun Fukuda, this vibrant flick was a departure from the city-stomping Godzilla epics helmed by the renowned Ishiro Honda. Mothra, along with her ever-present tiny twin priestesses, also joins in on the proceedings as a substantial number of her Infant Island worshippers are forced into slave labor by the bad guys. Fan fave Kumi Mizuno gives her most revealing performance as a scantily-clad native. D: Fukuda. C: Akira Takarada, Mizuno, Toru Watanabe, Hideo Sunazaka. TOHO

GODZILLA VS. THE SMOG MONSTER (J 1971, US 1972) *** A movie with a message, as an environmentally-conscious Godzilla has his hands full with a polluted pile of goop named Hedorah. Following on the heels of the tyke-friendly GODZILLA'S REVENGE, this cautionary tale was a jarring shift from the lighthearted fare to which fans had become accustomed. Director Yoshimitsu Banno infused elements of animation, psychedelica, experimental filmmaking, and the quasi-hip music of the era to create a strikingly atypical G flick. Hedorah, itself, is quite the oddity. It changes form on a whim (from tadpole to quadruped to flying saucer to biped) and spews corrosive sludge spitballs. Needing pollution to sustain, an opportunistic Hedorah sucks in toxic fumes from factory smokestacks, then expels deadly sulfuric-acid smog. You'll swear you've been inhaling secondhand smoke of a peculiar nature when you witness the Big G use his atomic breath as a means of jet propulsion to go airborne. No kidding: Godzilla can fly! The ambitious Banno plotted out a 3-D sequel for the IMAX format a few years back. Unfortunately, the project couldn't get adequate financial support. AKA: GODZILLA VS. HEDORAH. D: Banno. C: Akira Yamauchi, Toshie Kimura, Hiroyuki Kawase, Toshio Shibaki. TOHO

GODZILLA VS. SPACE GODZILLA (J 1994, US 1999) ***½ Unmitigated fun, as terrestrial Godzilla spars with his interstellar equal, an unwieldy look-alike with large crystalline growths sprouting from its shoulders. Seems that a few "G-cells" were carried into space (Mothra or Biollante are possible suspects) and sucked into a black hole. Out popped a bad-tempered Godzilla clone with an instinctive dislike of the Lizard King. Visually satisfying, as Koichi Kawakita's special effects pyrotechnics explode off the screen. There's also a modified version of Moguera, the huge robot from THE MYSTERIANS (1957). Now more of a combat vehicle, it's loaded to the max with lasers, grenade missiles, and a drill. The well-crafted narrative deftly delves into the complexities of our main characters. Hence, we get better acquainted with Miki Saegusa, the gifted telepath from the Heisei Era of G films. Miki (Megumi Odaka) has developed telekinetic powers and shares a special bond with

"Little Godzilla," last observed as a baby dinosaur in GODZILLA VS. MECHAGODZILLA II. Yeah, the mischievous creature is goofy-looking, but subteen viewers will love him. A bit of island adventure – and guest appearances by Mothra and the Shobijin fairies – are thrown in for good measure. This "long-necked" variation of Godzilla, with thunder thighs and elongated tail, is particularly imposing. D: Kensho Yamashita. C: Jun Hashizume, Odaka, Akira Emoto, Zenkichi Yoneyama, Kenji Sahara. TOHO

GODZILLA VS. THE THING (J 1964, US 1964) **** The "Thing" in question is our insect friend, Mothra. On paper, one might presume, a moth (albeit a giant moth) wouldn't stand a chance against the formidable "King of the Monsters." Did you ever see a moth drawn to the glow of one of those backyard bug zappers? It ain't pretty. I'm thinkin' one blast of Godzilla's nuclear-powered breath and it's over, right? But that's why these vagaries are played out on the kaiju battlefield. A hellacious typhoon washes ashore Mothra's egg; coincidentally, you-know-who angrily emerges from the terra firma. Mama Mothra flies in from her island home, maternal instincts intact. Along for the ride are the stylishly-attired Ailienas, the miniature twin fairies we first met in MOTHRA (1961). The sinewy surprise Godzilla receives from Mothra's assiduous offspring is one of Japanese sci-fi's more incredible moments. And that's saying something. AKA: GODZILLA VS. MOTHRA, MOTHRA VS. GODZILLA. D: Ishiro Honda. C: Akira Takarada, Yuriko Hoshi, Hiroshi Koizumi, Yu Fujiki, Kenji Sahara. TOHO

GODZILLA'S REVENGE (J 1969, US 1971) **½ Much maligned in certain circles, GODZILLA'S REVENGE is nevertheless an important film. It's unapologetically the most kiddie-oriented Godzilla flick by far, and a great introduction for youngsters to the wacky world of daikaiju eiga. A little squirt named Ichiro (Tomonori Yazaki) is mercilessly taunted by a strangely expressive gang of school bullies. With his parents working long hours, the lonely lad escapes in his daydreams to Monster Island, where an emphatic Godzilla is forcing doughy son Minya to defend himself against significantly larger enemies. A sharp eye will recognize the extensive stock footage borrowed from SON OF GODZILLA, GODZILLA VS. THE SEA MONSTER, and other Toho sci-fi movies. In this dream scenario, Minya shrinks to Ichiro's size and the two share their woes. Minya is having bully problems of his own, as a pug-faced, turquoise terror known as Gabara delights in shocking the living doo-doo out of the tubby cherub. Ichiro screeches, squeaks, and scats his dialogue in the American version, and Minya sounds an awful lot like Goofy, the Disney character. Eisei Amamoto, the angular actor usually cast as an evil or seedy sort, excels as Ichiro's kindly, toy-inventor neighbor. Kumio Miyaguchi's groovy music score is an absolute trip! AKA: ALL MONSTERS ATTACK. D: Ishiro Honda. C: Yazaki, Amamoto, Sachio Sakai, Kazuo Suzuki, Kenji Sahara. TOHO

GOJIRA See GODZILLA, KING OF THE MONSTERS

GOKE, BODYSNATCHER FROM HELL (J 1968, US 1969) ***½ GOKE is an interesting little pic that's held in awe by a staunch legion of horror/sci-fi fans. An Air Japan flight en route to Osaka crash-lands in uninhabited, craggy terrain after a harrowing experience with a UFO. The surviving passengers are left without food or water, but that's the least of their worries. A fellow traveler, possessed by a vicious alien life form, has turned into a bloodsucking vampire-type. The dude's forehead is actually forged open in order for the extraterrestrial goo to seep its way deep inside his cranium! Talk about a splitting headache. Meanwhile, our stranded protagonists squabble, and try to stay alive. Unfortunately, director Hajime Sato helmed only six features in his lifetime, and this was his last. AKA: BODY SNATCHER FROM HELL. D: Sato. C: Teruo Yoshida, Tomomi Sato, Hideo Ko, Eizo Kitamura. SHOCHIKU

GORATH (J 1962, US 1964) ***½ It's a shame that more people haven't seen this absorbing account of a runaway star on a straight path toward Earth. Rarely does this underrated gem show up on TV, and a legitimate DVD release in the States has yet to emerge. Scientists devise a plan to move our planet out of harm's way by igniting atomic-powered jet thrusters at the South Pole. Problem is, the dang star is sucking up cosmic debris, expanding, and getting too close for comfort. Lightning crackles, ocean levels dramatically rise, and mountains crumble. It ranks as one of the legendary Eiji Tsuburaya's top special effects efforts. This third film in Ishiro Honda's outer space trilogy (preceded by THE MYSTERIANS and BATTLE IN OUTER SPACE) again emphasizes the director's belief that mankind will ultimately work together, when necessary, to ensure world peace. The thoughtful dialogue was penned by Takeshi Kimura, who also scripted the Honda classic, ATTACK OF THE MUSHROOM PEOPLE. Producer

Tomoyuki Tanaka insisted that a giant monster be included in the movie to boost ticket sales. Those scenes, featuring a flabby walrus named Magma, were edited out of the U.S. version. D: Honda. C: Ryo Ikebe, Yumi Shirakawa, Takashi Shimura, Kumi Mizuno, Akira Kubo. TOHO

GORE FROM OUTER SPACE (J 2001, US 2004) **½ Oddly enough, there's no gore in GORE FROM OUTER SPACE. However, this unusual sci-fi/horror/comedy does include alien abduction, headless schoolgirls, kung fu fighting, flying houses, and an unexpected song or two. Sentenced to death on a murder rap, Satomi Kurahashi (Hitomi Miwa) recounts an inconceivable tale of woe on her way to the electric chair. Amongst the confusion: Satomi claims her daughter was kidnapped; her husband swears they never had a child. After awhile, it's hard to distinguish reality from fantasy. Aliens appear on Earth – assuming human form – with the intent of breeding with the populace. A daffy psychic and a couple of idiosyncratic FBI agents try to sort it all out. A sequel to the hit horror flick CRAZY LIPS, director Hirohisa Sasaki keeps things moving at a steady clip. Hiroshi Takahashi (THE RING) authored the script. D: Sasaki. C: Miwa, Sadao Abe, Hiroshi Abe, Aimi Nakamura. NIKKATSU/OMEGA/OZ

GREAT YOKAI WAR, THE (J 2005, US 2005) *** Deeply revered in Japanese folklore, yokai are mystical curiosities, often bizarre in appearance, with a proclivity for playing tricks on unsuspecting humankind. When school lad Tadashi is tapped to be the Kirin Rider – "protector of all things good" – he finds himself reluctantly leading a hodgepodge of ancient spirits into battle against a powerful, vile enemy. The evildoers are ruthlessly melding innocent yokai with society's discarded junk to make monstrous mechanical menaces. The yokai nation assembles, and man, they're a sight to see! Some bear resemblance to people, others to animals. All of the tools of the special effects trade – CGI, suitmation, stop-motion, puppetry, makeup, props, prosthetics – are pulled out to present such diverse yokai as a long-tongued umbrella, a properly-plated block of tofu, and a paper sliding door inset with copious, watchful eyes. Particularly impressive is the rendering of the Rokurokubi, a chambermaid whose sinuous neck stretches on . . . and on . . . and on . . . Director Takashi Miike, working with his biggest budget to date, lets his active imagination run wild. The film has drawn comparisons to Hayao Miyazaki's anime classic SPIRITED AWAY for the sheer number of spirits that come and go. Really, though, each has its own unique feel. D: Miike. C: Ryunosuke Kamiki, Hiroyuki Miyasako, Mai Takahashi, Masomi Kondo, Sadawo Abe. KADOKAWA

GREEN SLIME, THE (J 1968, US 1969) **½ The champagne flows freely as the crew of the Gamma III space station triumphantly celebrate after blasting apart an earthbound asteroid. The revelry, however, is short-lived as a small dab of green gunk from a piece of the asteroid has leeched onto one of our heroes. The goop mutates into one-eyed, tentacled monsters with a propensity for discharging lethal bolts of electricity. The disagreeable buggers can also propagate new creatures from their spilt blood, so weapons are out of the question. Meanwhile, the two major dudes in charge (Robert Horton and Richard Jaeckel) vie for the affection of Gamma's alluring doctor (portrayed by Bond girl Lucianna Paluzzi). A co-production between TOEI and

MGM, with a Japanese crew and a Western cast. Certainly, it's colorful and quirky. Director Kinji Fukasaku would go on to make the outrageous MESSAGE FROM SPACE. The film's 'outta' sight' theme song, played as the opening credits roll, gives you a good idea of where this thing is heading. D: Fukasaku. C: Horton, Jaeckel, Paluzzi, Bud Widom, William Ross. TOEI/MGM

GUNHED (J 1989, US 1996) **½ An early special effects vehicle for Koichi Kawakita, later to gain notice for his exploits in the Heisei Era Godzilla films. Thirteen years have passed since a battalion of piloted combat robots (or "mecha") infiltrated a private Pacific isle to prevent super computer Kyron-5 from eradicating the planet. Results of the intervention – though obviously positive – were unknown until now, when a rag-tag outfit of techno-bandits, searching for a precious element, find the island in ruins. Danger still lurks as Kyron-5's automated defense system remains up and running. One of the damaged mecha, a GUNHED unit, is reconditioned and thrown into the fray. The 30-foot-tall battle bot can transfer from upright mode to tank mode, contains ample artillery, and possesses a surprising gift of gab. The mission's new priority? Getting out of the friggin' place alive. Of interest: Masato Harada, the pic's director, had his name removed from the U.S. release when he learned it would be dubbed rather than subtitled. D: Harada. C: Masahiro Takashima, Brenda Bakke, Yujin Harada, Aya Enyoji. TOHO

H

H-MAN, THE (J 1958, US 1959) ***½ Japanese film noir – in color – with a healthy dose of admonitory sci-fi. A rain-drenched Tokyo is besieged by radioactive ooze creatures with the capacity to convert helpless humans into instant puddles of goo. Police detectives get suspicious when folks start disappearing, their clothes piled in a heap on the ground. They turn their attentions to a local nightclub singer (Yumi Shirakawa) whose connection to a missing mobster is believed to be crucial to solving the mystery. But, heck, it's only a matter of time before the liquidy entities (victims of H-bomb tests, we learn) are seeping from the city's sewer system and dissolving its denizens in front of our very eyes. Surely, Eiji Tsuburaya and his effects team had a blast creating such startling images. Striking just the right balance of atmosphere, mood, and suspense, THE H-MAN is among Ishiro Honda's finest directorial efforts. D: Honda. C: Shirakawa, Kenji Sahara, Akihiko Hirata, Koreya Senda, Yoshio Tsuchiya. TOHO

HALF HUMAN (J 1955, US 1958) * Director Ishiro Honda's next daikaiju eiga after GODZILLA, KING OF THE MONSTERS – a retelling of the Abominable Snowman saga – has rarely been seen in its intended form since the early 1960s due to depictions of native folk now deemed politically incorrect. What remains is the heavily-edited, 63-minute U.S. revision, which features noted actor John Carradine as an anthropologist touting the discovery of an imposing apelike creature in the Japanese Alps to his academic buddies back in the States. Normally peaceful, our furry (yet balding) friend seeks retribution when his son is accidentally gunned down by exploitative, traveling-circus types. Unfortunately, the film's brevity (and reliance on gratuitous narration) thwarts any possibility of sustainable drama. I'm guessing that the original version is, literally, a different story. Shot in black-and-white, a colorized print is said to have surfaced in the mid-1990s. AKA: HALF HUMAN: THE STORY OF THE ABOMINABLE SNOWMAN. D: Honda, Kenneth Crane. C: Carradine, Akira Takarada, Akemi Nigishi, Momoko Kochi. TOHO

HELLDRIVER (J 2011, US 2010) ** You had to figure that Sushi Typhoon, foremost purveyors of slop-and-glop cinema, would inevitably jump in with their own insane take on zombie movies. Yoshihiro Nishimura, director of the maniacal films MUTANT GIRLS SQUAD and TOKYO GORE POLICE – and special effects makeup man extraordinaire – gets the call and predictably assaults the viewer with a surfeit of surging blood and severed body parts. Nishimura also has a totally warped sense of humor. We witness a neonate zombie launched from the womb in attack mode and it's not out of place. Our twisted tale begins when a meteorite crashes in Japan, unleashing a toxic ash that turns the northern half of the country into the walking dead. A young gal named Kika, an experimental android with a convenient chainsaw sword, is sent into the infected sector to rid of the zombie queen, a despicable sort who also happens to be Kika's psycho mom. This is really, really weird stuff – and unconventional. The opening credits don't appear until we're nearly 50 minutes into the flick. Made its debut at the Austin Fantastic Fest in 2010, ahead of its 2011 Japanese release. D: Nishimura. C: Yumiko Hara, Eihi Shiina, Yurei Yanagi, Kazuko Namioka, Minoru Torihada,

Taka Guadalcanal, Mizuki Kusumi. NIKKATSU/SUSHI TYPHOON/SOMETHING CREATION

HELLEVATOR: THE BOTTLED FOOLS (J 2004, US 2004) *** Unusual indie movie about a futuristic world comprised solely of levels. The only means of getting to desired locations (home, work, shopping, etc.) is by way of spacious transport elevators. Luchino, a 17-year-old schoolgirl with mind-reading capabilities, sneaks a smoke – forbidden in this society – and bolts to a nearby elevator to avoid prosecution. She comes across some mighty strange folks: rotelike businessmen, a little girl with a human brain for a pet, and a quiet fellow in shades. It's all presided over by a neat, efficient elevator attendant. The situation gets dicey when a pair of psychotic prisoners are hauled aboard; they elude their captors and the blood starts spurting freely. First-time director Hiroki Yamaguchi injects a plot twist near the film's close that smartly wraps things up. A claustrophobic viewing experience, for sure, as most of the action takes place in an elevator. But it's a *BIG* elevator. D: Yamaguchi. C: Rukino Fujisaki, Ryosuke Koshiba, Yuuko Takarada, Ikuma Saisho, Kae Minamu. ARIES/ONLY HEARTS/WEVCO

HUMAN VAPOR, THE (J 1960, US 1964) **½ Last in a trio of classic Toho sci-fi flicks concerning characters in a state of flux, following THE H-MAN (radioactive mutation) and THE SECRET OF THE TELEGIAN (wave teleportation). Humble librarian Mizuno (Yoshio Tsuchiya) acquires the ability to transform himself into a thick, gaseous mist as a result of a scientific experiment gone haywire. Mizuno goes cuckoo, robbing banks (and offing a lot of cops) to finance the career of a fetching dancer. Tsuchiya, as always, is in fine form. His performance is even more compelling in the Japanese version (***) as the American release was re-edited to reflect Mizuno's point of view, eliminating an air of mystery carefully crafted by director Ishiro Honda. The tight scripting is by Takeshi Kimura, who specialized in writing the serious Toho tokusatsu films of the era. (Shinichi Sekizawa was favored for the breezier fare.) Mizuno's metamorphosis into the "vapor man" is skillfully executed by FX guru Eiji Tsuburaya. Kaiju eiga enthusiasts will want to check out THE HUMAN VAPOR, though it's difficult to find. D: Honda. C: Tatsuya Mihashi, Kaoru Yachigusa, Tsuchiya, Keiko Sata. TOHO

I-J

INVADERS FROM SPACE (J 1957, US 1964) ** Leapin' lizards! Acrobatic salamander men from the planet Kulamon are endangering Earth with their dancin', prancin' ways. Fear not. Our far-out friends from the High Council of the Emerald Planet have dispatched Starman, the superhero dude with the Olympic gymnast moves, to rescue our sorry butts. This is actually the second of four preposterous flicks to feature the intergalactic good guy. He has his work cut out for him in this one, as the sinister Kulamonians utilize radioactive breath, high-decibel sound waves, and germ warfare in an attempt to destroy, and then rebuild, our unwary world. Fortunately, our flamboyant hero is (as we've come to learn) "made of the strongest steel." Lensed in black-and-white, the whole thing has the feel of American serials of the 1930s and 1940s – with a Far East spin. D: Teruo Ishii, Akira Mitsuwa, Koreyoshi Akasada. C: Ken Utsui, Sachihiro Ohsawa, Junko Ikeuchi, Minako Yamada. FUJI/SHINTOHO

INVASION OF ASTRO-MONSTER See GODZILLA VS. MONSTER ZERO

INVASION OF THE NEPTUNE MEN (J 1961, US 1964) ** Early starring turn for Shinichi "Sonny" Chiba, later to emerge as a martial arts cinema celeb in the 1970s. Chiba dons white tights, cape, an oversized helmet, and sun visor here to play the raygun-toting champion of justice, Space Chief. When metallic, coneheaded aliens threaten Earth, our hero is there in a jiff, riding in first-class comfort in a jet-propelled luxury sedan! The Neptunians' curious takeover strategy includes changing our climate, and reversing the electrical current of clocks, trains, and phonographs so they run backwards. More drastic measures involve blowing up our nuclear reactors and intimidating a group of dorky schoolboys who idolize the aloof Space Chief. One of a number of black-and-white superhero films from Japan to make it to U.S. shores in the mid-1960s. This may be the best of the lot, with solid special effects, a nice sense of continuity, and a deluge of incredulous science babble. Go ahead and get your geek on. D: Koji Ota. C: Chiba, Kappei Matsumoto, Shinjiro Ebara, Mitsue Komiya, Ryuko Minakami. TOEI

K

K-20: THE FIEND WITH TWENTY FACES (J 2008, US 2008) ***½ Possibly the coolest Japanese superhero flick ever concocted, though our title character – draped in black – is essentially an evil Robin Hood of sorts who robs from the rich but *doesn't* give to the poor. Set in 1949 Japan, in an alternate realm where World War II never existed, the masked marauder (with cape a-swirlin') creates chaos when the country's ruling power tries to implement physicist Nikola Tesla's technology to harness an unlimited amount of wireless energy. An adroit circus performer (Takeshi Kaneshiro of RETURNER and HOUSE OF FLYING DAGGERS) takes the fall for K-20 and sets out to clear his name. Also in the mix: a famous detective, who has long pursued the elusive K-20, and a well-heeled heiress, whose eccentricities provide the film with its lighter moments. Visually arresting, with dirigibles and gyro-copters hovering above a dark, yet futuristic, metropolis. The influence of Tim Burton's Batman pics and Marvel's recent cinematic output is obvious but welcomed. K-20 is a prominent figure in Japanese lit, with many a clever adventure. Consequently, the script has enough twists and turns to keep even the casual viewer intrigued. D: Shimako Sato. C: Kaneshiro, Takako Matsu, Toru Nakamura, Ryohei Abe, Yuki Ima. NIPPON TELEVISION NETWORK/ROBOT COMMUNICATIONS/TOHO

KAMEN RIDER: THE FIRST See MASKED RIDER: THE FIRST

KING KONG ESCAPES (J 1967, US 1968) *** Whew! They sure don't make 'em like this anymore. Goofy, yes, but colorful and immensely entertaining. Miscreants kidnap the legendary Kong from his idyllic island abode, as his muscle is needed to retrieve a coveted, but dangerous, radioactive mother lode. To the rescue is the unflappable Commander Nelson, portrayed by the sturdy Rhodes Reason. Meanwhile, a horned-up Kong is hot and bothered by a perky blonde with a squeaky voice (Linda Miller). Based on an American cartoon of the time, this is fabulous, chest-pounding frolic. Toho favorite Eisei Amamoto – he of the wiry physique – delightfully hams it up, playing an international bad guy. Kong (looking less shaggy than in his 1963 outing against Godzilla) grapples with a nondescript sea snake, the leaping dino Gorosaurus, and Mechani-Kong, a silvery robot replication of the big ape. I'm thinkin' that a Mechagodzilla vs. Mechani-Kong matchup would have been a clankin'-fun flick, but it was never considered. Hey, it's not too late . . . D: Ishiro Honda. C: Reason, Akira Takarada, Mie Hama, Miller, Amamoto. TOHO/RANKIN-BASS

KING KONG VS. GODZILLA (J 1962, US 1963) **½ A marquee matchup, for sure, and still the highest-attended Godzilla film to this day in Japan. Panic ensues when the King of the Monsters thaws out from an iceberg's subzero hold. Kong (an actor in a plush gorilla suit) fights off an enormous, oleaginous octopus on his South Seas island home, gets drunk on the natives' red berry juice, and passes out. Hungry for publicity, the reps of a pharmaceutical company capture the sleeping ape and head for Japan. Kong, of course, escapes. The iconic behemoths eventually tangle atop Mt. Fuji in an all-too-brief but comical scuffle involving a ton o' rocks. The first G movie in color, the Japanese version (***) is a light satire on the excesses of commercialism. Much is lost in the U.S. release, which replaces key segments of dialogue with newsroom commentary from a United Nations reporter and a natural history "expert." For years, it was believed that Godzilla arose as the victor in the original Japanese pic, and Kong prevailed in the American unspooling. But that's simply not the case. D: Ishiro Honda. C: Tadao Takashima, Yu Fujiki, Kenji Sahara, Mie Hama, Akiko Wakabayashi. TOHO

L

L: CHANGE THE WORLD (J 2008, US 2009) **** Comfortably veering from fright fare to sci-fi territory is this exhilarating spin-off of the first two DEATH NOTE films. Ironically, it's directed by well-known horror helmsman Hideo Nakata. L, the subdued dude with the pronounced slouch, is back. But he has only 23 days to live – and 22 days to save the world from a bioterrorist faction aiming to eliminate most of humanity with a virus 100 times stronger than Ebola. The race is on to secure an antidote. L, computer prowess intact, gets unlikely help from a young boy - the only survivor of a Thai village decimated by the virus - and a 12-year-old girl whose scientist father had once created a remedy for the lethal bug. Kenichi Matsuyama is engaging as the enigmatic, quirky L. A big plus is the pic's tight dubbing. And while it helps to be familiar with the source material – be it manga, anime, or film – it isn't necessary. AKA: DEATH NOTE L: CHANGE THE WORLD, DEATH

NOTE III. D: Nakata. C: Matsuyama, Narushi Fukuda, Mayuko Fukuda, Kimihiko Nikaido, Youki Kudo. NIKKATSU/L FILM PARTNERS

LAST DAYS OF PLANET EARTH, THE See PROPHECIES OF NOSTRADAMUS

LAST DINOSAUR, THE (J 1977, US 1977) *** An unforeseen contingent of daikaiju-starved fans of the 1970s greeted this modest dino flick with arms wide open. It's an intriguing collaboration between the irrepressible gang from Tsuburaya Productions and Rankin-Bass, the nutty outfit best known for stop-motion puppetry classics like RUDOLPH THE RED-NOSED REINDEER and THE YEAR WITHOUT A SANTA CLAUS. This particular undertaking, however, is strictly a live-action endeavor, augmented with men-in-suit prehistoric creatures running hither and yon. Rough-hewn Richard Boone (HAVE GUN, WILL TRAVEL) plays Masten Thrust, a wealthy oil tycoon/big-game hunter/skirt chaser whose drilling company discovers a hidden valley beneath the polar ice cap. It's a world teeming with dinosaurs and inhabited by, oddly enough, Japanese cave people. Thrust heads up an expedition party, and it's not long before he's obsessed with hunting down and killing a fierce, elusive T-Rex. (It's actually the same T-Rex costume used in the bewildering ATTACK OF THE SUPER MONSTERS.) Joan Van Ark (KNOTS LANDING) portrays an award-winning photographer who surprisingly has the hots for the rude, crude, lewd Thrust. Also on hand is the tongue-tied Bunta, a Maasai tracker played by 6-foot-10 ex-NBAer, Luther Rackley. Originally intended for the big screen in the States but wound up on television as the ABC

Movie of the Week. Renowned jazz singer Nancy Wilson classes things up by crooning the film's poignant opening theme. D: Tsugunobu "Tom" Kotani, Alexander Grasshoff. C: Boone, Van Ark, Steven Keats, Rackley, Tetsu Nakamura, Masumi Sekiya, Carl Hansen, William Ross. TSUBURAYA PRODUCTIONS/RANKIN-BASS

LAST WAR, THE (J 1961, US 1964) *** Released at the height of the Cold War, this end-of-the-world downer packs quite the emotional wallop. Tensions mount as two unnamed superpowers (obviously the U.S. and Russia) repeatedly ignore United Nations warnings to play nice. Amidst it all, a tight-knit Japanese family deals with the impending threat of nuclear devastation. Ultimately, the bombs start falling, and several major cities – including Tokyo – are reduced to rubble; Eiji Tsuburaya's special effects destruction is painfully realistic. Frankie Sakai (the waggish reporter in MOTHRA) is exceptional as the doomed family's patriarch, though gruff-sounding dubbing diminishes the subtleties of his performance inherent in the Japanese version. Sad, solemn stuff, and still stirringly effective. D: Shue Matsubayashi. C: Sakai, Akira Takarada, Yuriko Hoshi, Nobuka Otawa, Yumi Shirakawa. TOHO

LATITUDE ZERO (J 1969, US 1970) **½ Get this: Here's a tokusatsu pic filmed in English – but then dubbed in Japanese for viewers in the Land of the Rising Sun. Amongst a backdrop of submersible sci-fi hijinks, genre stalwarts Akira Takarada and Akihiko Hirata interestingly go outside their comfort zones, earnestly pronouncing their lines in Anglican tongue. (Takarada does well but sorta sounds like a Frenchman. Hirata, well, he gives it his best shot.) Our adventure begins when a bathysphere mishap catapults an oceanographer, a geologist, and a reporter to a secret underwater city ruled by the nattily-dressed Captain McKenzie (who is played with restraint by the distinguished Hollywood actor, Joseph Cotton). It's a marvy place where scientists from around the world can conduct research free from scrutiny. The diabolical Dr. Malic (portrayed by Cesar Romero . . . the Joker!) does his darndest to undo the good captain's work by unleashing human-sized rats, mutant bats, and – I kid you not – a giant flyin' lion. This was to be director Ishiro Honda's highest-budgeted flick until U.S. investment in the film was withdrawn at the last minute, cutting financial resources in half. Nonetheless, the special effects are scintillating, and the miniatures craftsmanship is first-rate. Long sought after, LATITUDE ZERO remained in legal limbo due to a rights dispute until Tokyo Shock's much-anticipated 2007 DVD release. D: Honda. C: Cotten, Romero, Takarada, Richard Jaeckel, Masumi Okada, Patricia Medina, Linda Haynes. TOHO

LEGEND OF DINOSAURS, THE See THE LEGEND OF DINOSAURS AND MONSTER BIRDS

LEGEND OF DINOSAURS AND MONSTER BIRDS, THE (J 1977, US 1987) *1/2 The lengthy title is somewhat misleading as there's but one measly dinosaur and one friggin' monster bird in the whole doggone flick. The creatures in question – a soggy plesiosaur and a deranged pterodactyl – emerge near a Mt. Fuji lake to terrorize the local yokels. Picky eaters, though, these monsters. One bite of human folk, and they spit out the rest, leaving behind a sickening trail of severed heads, torsos, and bloodied body parts. It's no surprise that both are noticeably emaciated. Trying to make sense of it all are a determined geologist and his scuba-diving girlfriend. Masao Yagi's music score – a mix of smooth jazz, West Coast AOR, and disco – frequently jumps in at the unlikeliest of moments. Noteworthy for being the costliest production in Toei's history at the time of its release. AKA: THE LEGEND OF DINOSAURS. D: Junji Kurata. C: Tsunehiko Watase, Nobiko Sawa. TOEI

M

MAGIC SERPENT, THE (J 1966, US 1968) *** The classic saga of good vs. evil is played to the hilt in this lively sword-and-sorcery fantasy with a daikaiju twist. A young prince with mystical abilities seeks vengeance on the detestable dudes who slayed his parents and, later, his wise old ninja master. Using an ancient form of hocus pocus, our spry adversaries transform into giant creatures to fight for control of the noble prince's deposed kingdom. A spikey-backed, fire-breathing frog rumbles with our title subject, a water-sloshin' Reptilicus knockoff; also in on the fun is a bodacious big bird and a web-spouting, flying spider. And, no, your ears aren't deceiving you. The recognizable wails of Godzilla, Rodan, Mothra, and Ebirah were allegedly "borrowed" from Toho for the film's American release. Produced by Toei, the same people who dreamt up JOHNNY SOKKO AND HIS FLYING ROBOT. D: Tetsuya Yamauchi. C: Hiroki Matsukata, Tomo Ogawa, Ryutaro Otomo. TOEI

MAJIN See MAJIN, MONSTER OF TERROR

MAJIN, MONSTER OF TERROR (J 1966, US 1968) **½ The first in a trio of engrossing flicks with the mighty Majin, a 50-foot-high stone idol that comes alive to squash evildoers in feudal Japan. Samanosuke, a wicked warlord forces the peasants of a small village to construct a massive fortress. (Torturing the help is his favorite pastime.) Majin, embedded in a mountainside, is eventually hailed – with a measly 15 minutes left in the dang film! Oh well, better late than never. Resembling a sneering samurai and possessing a warrior's spirit, the relentless Majin proceeds to kick major bad-guy butt. It's worth the wait. Taking a break from Godzilla and other Toho projects, Akira Ifukube delivers a mood-drenched, memorable soundtrack. Presented in living color by Daiei, creators of that loveable tusked turtle, Gamera. AKA: DAIMAJIN, MAJIN. D: Kimiyoshi Yasuda. C: Miwa Takada, Yoshiko Aoyama, Jun Fukimaki, Ryutaro Gomi. DAIEI

MAJIN STRIKES AGAIN (J 1966, US 1999) **½ The final entry of the trilogy featuring the resilient Majin, an imposing stone statue that awakens to crush oppressive types in medieval Japan. Sticks closely to the formula of the previous entries: a mean tyrant brutalizes the locals, the locals pray for Majin's help, Majin appears a little over an hour into the flick to settle the score. This time, however, Majin (played, as always, with a perpetual grimace by Riki Hashimoto) methodically plods through a raging snowstorm as he mashes wrongdoers. Yoshiyuki Kuroda's effects work here is exemplary. Much of the story centers around four courageous boys, who trek to Majin's sacred resting place in the mountains to rescue their enslaved fathers. Oftentimes incredibly somber, but the MAJIN films always reward those who patiently await their gratifying conclusions. AKA: DAIMAJIN STRIKES AGAIN. D: Kazuo Mori. C: Hideki Ninomiya, Masahide Zizuka, Shinji Hori, Shiei Iizuka. DAIEI

MANSTER, THE (J 1959, US 1962) **½ Contrary to popular belief, two heads are *not* always better than one. That's the lesson learned in this curious little account of science gone horribly askew. Foreign newspaper correspondent Larry Stanford (Peter Dyneley) seeks out renegade Japanese scientist Robert Suzuki for an exclusive story but soon finds himself a subject of the madman's fiendish experiments. Oh, it all looks good in the beginning. Suzuki (Tetsu Nakamura) exposes a grateful Stanford to the pleasures of the Tokyo nightlife; both the sake and the geisha girls are plentiful. Problem is, that itty-bitty injection of serum administered by Suzuki has left our muddled reporter with a hairy paw, an eyeball bulging from his shoulder, and ultimately, a second noggin! A murderous rampage ensues. Stanford's concerned wife arrives in Japan and is understandably dismayed by her husband's inappropriate behavior. A U.S.-Japanese co-production, THE MANSTER is an underrated, effective monster-on-the-loose chiller filmed in simple black-and-white. AKA: THE MANSTER: HALF-MAN, HALF-MONSTER. D: George P.Breakston, Kenneth G. Crane. C: Dyneley, Jane Hylton, Nakamura, Teri Zimmern. UNITED ARTISTS

MANSTER: HALF-MAN, HALF-MONSTER, THE See THE MANSTER

MASKED RIDER: THE FIRST (J 2005, US 2007) *** Based on the classic KAMEN RIDER television series, which has aired in Japan in various incarnations since 1971. Longtime fans may disagree with a few of the variations made for the widescreen adaptation, but these are minor quibbles. This is a heckuva fun thrill ride. Terrorists kidnap promising grad student Takeshi Hongo (Masaya Kikawada) and turn him into a bug-eyed, motorcycling cyborg. World domination is the objective, but young Takeshi breaks free of the mental hold of his captors. Another cyborg – sent to contain Takeshi – also regains his senses, and the daring duo display some nifty martial arts moves and madcap motorcycle derring-do while battling the bad guys. Though the TV show was geared for kids, this film aims to appeal to all ages. (At times, it's rather dark). A sequel followed, but has yet to be released in the States. AKA: KAMEN RIDER: THE FIRST. D: Takao Nagaishi. C: Kikawada, Hassei Takano, Rena Komine, Hiroshi Miyauchi. TOEI

MATANGO See ATTACK OF THE MUSHROOM PEOPLE

MEATBALL MACHINE (J 2005, US 2006) **½ Not your typical romantic tale. Boy meets girl, they fall head-over-heels in love, then girl gets infected by a slimy alien parasite. Their first fight is a real ripsnorter, as girl changes into a strange, flesh-eating creature bestowed with biomechanic artillery. Others are afflicted in like manner, as the pesky extraterrestrial pests implant themselves within unfortunate humans to do battle. To the winner go the spoils – literally – as the loser is eaten! The merging of alloy and epidermis brings to mind Shinya Tsukamoto's Tetsuo films, as rubber cables and metal tentacles overwhelm the unlucky victims to create hunk-of-junk cyborgs. Gore aficionados will appreciate the endless stream of blood, goop, and slop bestrewn across the screen. The cyborgs were designed by Keita Amemiya, the mastermind of the ZEIRAM pics. D: Yudai Yamaguchi, Yamamoto. C: Issei Takahashi, Aoba Kawai. KING RECORD COMPANY

MECHANICAL VIOLATOR HAKAIDER (J 1995, US 2001) *** Yet another cool film from director Keita Amemiya, the imaginative mind behind MOON OVER TAO and the ZEIRAM flicks. For those unaware, Hakaider is the purely evil humanoid from the seminal Japanese superhero television show, KIKAIDER. Clad in black, the motorcycle-ridin', gun-totin' Hakaider cruises into Jesus Town, a false utopia overseen by a pensive yet domineering despot named Gurjev. Relying on instinct, our title character fights alongside rebel forces to overthrow Gurjev's tyrannical rule. Many old-school tokusatsu fans were unsettled by the depiction of Kikaider's arch-rival as an anti-hero. However, we learn early on that Haikaider's memory is foggy after years of imprisonment, leaving him unsure of his life's purpose. Works for me. As expected, Amemiya's action scenes are well-executed, especially in the harrowing motorcycle maneuvers involving Jesus Town's heavily-armed security detail. The closing encounter between Hakaider and "Michael," the sleek automaton responsible for "enforcing" Gurjev's tenet of peace and love, clangs with clatter-filled chaos. AKA: ROBOMAN HAKAIDER. D:

Amemiya. C: Yuji Kishimoto, Mai Hosho, Yasuaki Honda, Satoshi Kurihara. TOEI

MESSAGE FROM SPACE (J 1978, US 1978) ** And that message is loud and clear: Outer space is a cruel, crazy, beautiful scene. A grand expanse graced by glittering interstellar fireflies, yet terrorized by silver-skinned aliens with no qualms about obliterating populated planets. One such world, nonviolent Jillucia, is on the verge of annihilation. A sundry collection of folks are summoned (by magically-propelled glowing walnuts!) to throw down the gauntlet. The oft-inebriated General Garuda (Vic Morrow of COMBAT! fame) and his long-winded little robot buddy, Beba, are among those who reluctantly heed the call. Heavily influenced by STAR WARS, which was immensely popular in Japan at the time. Swift celestial chases and spirited swordwork abound. Something, though, you won't see in STAR WARS: the Jillucians' astonishing space vessel, a 16th-century galleon – complete with oars – sailing effortlessly amidst the stars. Director Kinji Fukasaku's random forays into sci-fi (he also helmed THE GREEN SLIME and VIRUS) are, indeed, off-kilter affairs. D: Fukasaku. C: Morrow, Shinichi "Sonny" Chiba, Philip Casnoff, Peggy Lee Brennan. TOEI

MESSAGE FROM OUTER SPACE See SWORDS OF THE SPACE ARK

MIGHTY JACK (J 1968, US 1986) **½ Here's some more escapism from Tsuburaya Productions, the company started by Toho special effects trailblazer, Eiji Tsuburaya. Actually a Japanese TV series, MIGHTY JACK was a personal fave of Eiji; two episodes of the show were combined to create this feature-length film for American audiences. What's formed is a decent little cloak-and-dagger caper with sci-fi elements. Mighty Jack is the name of a top-secret group of operatives brought together to fight a malevolent international outfit known as "Q." Headquartered inside a giant iceberg, the cunning reprobates have invented deep-freeze weaponry utilizing a non-melting type of ice! Our protagonists, traveling aboard a slick jet/submarine hybrid, follow in rapid pursuit. Unlike most of the Tsuburaya fare, MIGHTY JACK was targeted more toward adult viewers. D: Kazuho "Pete" Mitsuta. C: Hideaki Nitani, Naoko Kubo, Hiroshi Minami. TSUBURAYA PRODUCTIONS

MIKADROID: ROBOKILL BENEATH DISCO CLUB LAYLA (J 1991, US 2006) **½ Wow, that's some title. And who knew that disco was alive and well in Japan in the early 1990s? Sadly, the same can't be said for several of the patrons of a hot new Tokyo nightclub, who meet an untimely demise at the steely hands of Mikadroid – a half-man, half-machine menace with an itchy trigger finger. Seems that the Japanese were busy developing cyborg super soldiers near the end of World War II in a secret lab located – you guessed it – beneath the happenin' disco club. Mikadroid is inadvertently reactivated after 45 years of slumber, and the imposing, copper-hued robot goes on an unprovoked killing spree. And dang, the thing is equipped with a full friggin' arsenal: short-range rifle, explosives, military saber, even a parachute! Shinji Higuchi, in his initial outing as a special effects director, surely had fun with this one. Not your usual Toho sci-fi movie, but still a worthwhile diversion. D: Tomoo Haraguchi. C: Yoriko Doguchi, Yuki Yoshida, Hiroshi Atsumi, Kiyoshi Kurosawa, Masako Takeda. TOHO

MIRROR MAN: REFLEX (J 2006, US 2006) **½ MIRROR MAN was one of the numerous short-lived, yet indelible, tokusatsu programs broadcast on Japanese television in the early 1970s. The premise: oversized instigators from another dimension enter our world and Mirror Man shows up to save our heinies. This full-length feature, compiled from a three-part, direct-to-DVD series, finds a troubled fella named Akira Kageyama (Ryo Karato) transmitting warnings of impending doom on an internet radio station. When a trio of outrageous "demon monsters" materialize, Akira transforms – via a magic mirror's emerald glow – into the prodigious Mirror Man. This time around, our hero dons a green-and-silver metallic suit similar to the design seen in the original manga. Big props to director Kazuya Konaka for the vivacious, tightly-rehearsed sparring that follows. Created by Tsuburaya Productions, the folks best known for ULTRAMAN. (This, however, has a much darker tone.) It's pretty tough to track down a copy of this underappreciated pic, but it's definitely worth the search. Noboyuki Ishida, who portrayed Mirror Man on the small screen, appears as Akira's bro. AKA: MIRRORMAN: REFLEX. D: Konaka. C: Karato, Yuko Ito, Miku Ishida. TSUBURAYA PRODUCTIONS

MIRRORMAN: REFLEX See MIRROR MAN: REFLEX

MONSTER FROM A PREHISTORIC PLANET (J 1967, US 1967) ** "Gappa angry!" warn the frightened natives of Obelisk Island, a primitive paradise in the South Pacific. But, sorry to say, nobody's listening. An expedition party has captured a freshly-hatched Gappa (a half-bird, half-reptile oddity) with the intent of turning the cacophonous critter into a major tourist draw back in Japan. Bad move. Clearly peeved, the giant-sized Mama and Papa Gappa soar to Tokyo to get the kid – and do some serious city-smashing in the process. But don't fret. This "family film" has a heartfelt finale. And, as far as South Seas island adventures go, there are all the basic necessities: sacramental tribal dances, idol worship, an erupting volcano, etc. Unfortunately, most of the existing prints of this oft-televised flick are somewhat murky. AKA: GAPPA, THE TRIPHIBIAN MONSTER. D: Haruyasu Noguchi. C: Tamio Kawaji, Yoko Yamamoto, Yuji Okada, Koji Wada, Tatsuya Fuji. NIKKATSU

MONSTER X STRIKES BACK: ATTACK THE G8 SUMMIT (J 2008, US 2009) *** A mere 41 years after terrorizing Japan in THE X FROM OUTER SPACE, Guilala – the latex lizard with the big ol' bug eyes – returns in this batty homage to 1960s' daikaiju movies. The G8 Summit, a gathering of major world leaders held in Hokkaido, is disrupted when the crash of a Mars space probe converts a cosmic spore into the contemptuous Guilala. The huge creature chortles heartily as Earth's mightiest nations fail miserably (and humorously) in their attempts to immobilize him. Luckily, a spunky gal reporter chances upon a small congregation near Lake Toya that worships the guardian deity, Take-Majin. Awakened by an absurd dance ritual, the

50-foot-tall golden idol promptly gets swept up in a rollicking smackdown with a flippant Guilala. Though some are critical of the film's histrionic political satire, there are quite a few laugh-out-loud moments. And director Minoru Kawasaki (THE WORLD SINKS EXCEPT JAPAN) isn't averse to throwing in an occasional burp, fart, or bad bout of diarrhea just for kicks. The noted actor/director/writer "Beat" Takeshi Kitano – "Vic Romano" to you MXC fans – is hilarious as the bewildered Take-Majin. D: Kawasaki. C: Natsuki Kato, Kazuki Kato, Kitano. SHOCHIKU

MONSTER ZERO See GODZILLA VS. MONSTER ZERO

MOON OVER TAO (J 1997, US 1999) *** Set amid the tumult of 16th-century Japan, this unrestrained sci-fi/fantasy flick from Keita Amemiya deftly demonstrates the director's ability to blend breakneck action with clever special effects. Kakugyo, an evil sorcerer, is manufacturing "super swords" made from the metal shell of a mysterious sphere from outer space. A disparate trio – Suiko the magical warrior monk, Hayate the adroit blade handler, and Renge the prepubescent beekeeper – set out for answers. Also checking out the situation are three expressionless alien chicks (all played by Yuko Moriyama, the star of Amemiya's ZEIRAM films) who have the inside scoop on the sphere's origin. Alas, it's too late. The Makaraga, an icky quadruped with a hankering for hemoglobin, is unleashed. Predictably, there's a spate of slicing and slitting in this one, guaranteeing a glut of severed limbs and spurting fluids. A weird mix, for sure, but it works. AKA: MOON OVER TAO – MAKARAGA. D: Amemiya. C: Toshiyuki Nagashima,

Hiroshi Abe, Sayaka Yoshino, Moriyama. BANDAI VISUAL/SHOCHIKU

MOON OVER TAO – MAKARAGA See MOON OVER TAO

MOTHRA (J 1961, US 1962) ***½ The multicolored giant moth's debut is a retreat from the weighty daikaiju films of the time, thanks in part to screenwriter Shinichi Sekizawa's predilection for light comedy, satire, and upbeat endings. We venture to funky Infant Island, where an inquisitive expedition team discovers a pair of teeny-tiny twin fairies called the Ailienas. The little ladies (played by the popular Japanese pop-singing duo, "the Peanuts") are swiped from their homeland by an avaricious entrepreneur and heartlessly exhibited for profit in Japan. Meanwhile, back on the island, squeaky-clean natives perform a ceremonial shake-and-shimmy, and a jumbo-sized egg cracks open. A puffy, brown caterpillar toddles out, swims to the mainland, encases itself in a cocoon on Tokyo Tower, and metamorphosizes into our flap-happy title bug. Cars roll and tumble down windblown city streets and buildings collapse as a persistent Mothra searches for her beloved Ailienas. Despite the destruction, this is a mellow little flick that's easy to adore. The cast (particularly Frankie Sakai in a comic role as a "bulldog" reporter) is excellent. Mothra would next be seen in 1964's GODZILLA VS. THE THING. D: Ishiro Honda. C: Sakai, Hiroshi Koizumi, Kyoko Kagawa, the Peanuts (Emi and Yumi Ito). TOHO

MOTHRA VS. GODZILLA See GODZILLA VS. THE THING

MUTANT GIRLS SQUAD (J 2010, US 2010) **½ A twisted tribute (kinda) to the X-Men movies, but saturated with a surplus of gore, glop, and splatter. Rin, an awkward 16-year-old schoolgirl, realizes she is a frickin' mutant when her hand suddenly morphs into a mechanical claw. Persecuted by society and pursued by the Japanese government, the shell-shocked teen falls in with a rancorous band of mutants known as the Hilko Clan. (The Hilkos were doing just fine, thank you, until those bothersome humans came along and ruined their good time.) Rin's new pals, employing such unique hardware as breast swords and an anal chainsaw, take aim at a helpless populace. The hacking is incessant, with blood drenching everything in sight – even the camera lens. You wouldn't expect anything less from the prolific trio combining forces to direct this sick flick: Noboru Iguchi helmed MACHINE GIRL and ROBOGEISHA, Yoshihiro Nishimura created the special effects makeup for MEATBALL MACHINE and TOKYO GORE POLICE, and Tak Sakaguchi had memorable acting turns in ALIVE and VERSUS. These dudes are incredibly inventive in devising different ways to decapitate, split, and pulverize the heads of unfortunate folk. Those who applaud this outlandish style of cinema will find this film to be quite a lot of fun – and funny, too. D: Iguchi, Nishimura, Sakaguchi. C: Yumi Sugimoto, Yuko Takayama, Suzuka Morita, Sakaguchi. NIKKATSU/SUSHI TYPHOON/TOEI

MYSTERIANS, THE (J 1957, US 1959) **** The first Japanese science-fiction film shot in TohoScope, the widescreen format similar to CinemaScope. It's classic early Toho, a color-drenched spectacle with a torrent of exhilarating special effects from the master of disaster himself, Eiji Tsuburaya. Cape-wearing, helmeted aliens arrive on Earth under the guise of peace. But they really wish to conquer the planet and get their freak on with our women! The extraterrestrial horndogs set loose the giant robot Moguera – sort of a needle-nosed mole with rapid-fire eye lasers – and a rural village near Mt. Fuji is quickly demolished. The rest of the world is next. Can countries put aside their differences and band together to defeat the smug alien intruders? It's a favorite theme of director Ishiro Honda, not only explored here but in this pic's engrossing sequels, BATTLE IN OUTER SPACE and GORATH. Lots and lots of miniatures – jets, tanks, and flying saucers among 'em – get blown apart in this one. Sit back and enjoy the Showa! D: Honda. C: Kenji Sahara, Yumi Shirakawa, Momoko Kochi, Akihiko Hirata, Takashi Shimura. TOHO

N

NEGADON: THE MONSTER FROM MARS (J 2005, US 2006) *** Touted as the world's first computer-generated monster movie, although – at 27 minutes running time – it's more a showcase of the technological marvels of modern-day filmmaking. And despite the undeniable creepiness of CGI-rendered human beings, the visuals in this reverential nod to the golden era of daikaiju eiga are absolutely breathtaking. The story: A humongous rock formation – brought back from a Mars expedition – crashes on Earth. Out pops Negadon, a giant buglike creature that emits fiery laser strikes. Brilliant scientist Ryuichi Narasaki dusts off the Miroku Unit 2, a towering robot that flawlessly executes jumps and somersaults, and wields a useful appendage drill. The two titans face off in downtown Tokyo, and ultimately, outer space. Directed and written by newcomer Jun Awazu, the project took almost two-and-a-half years to complete. The Manga Corps DVD release includes an interview with Awazu, a "Making of Negadon" featurette, and several other surprises. Definitely deserves a look. D: Awazu. COMIX WAVE/STUDIO MAGARA

NEZULLA, THE RAT MONSTER (J 2002, US 2006) ** Finally, a creature feature for animal rights activists. Secret scientific experiments to immunize soldiers against bacterial warfare go dreadfully amiss when an ordinary lab rat is transformed into a 7-foot-tall raging rodent. To make matters worse, harmful microorganisms are unintentionally released, infecting the general public. A rough-and-ready band of yahoos infiltrate the abandoned research facility, attempting to secure a blood sample from our mutated title character in order to create a life-saving vaccine. It ain't gonna be easy, as the vicious varmint is impervious to bullets. (I'm thinkin' all along that rat poison or a giant mousetrap might do the trick, but what do I know?) The elusive Nezulla doesn't get a ton of screen time; director Kanta Tagawa chooses to build suspense by implying that the hideous abhorrence is constantly lurking around the next corner. Sort of the "when you least expect it, expect it" approach. Gained notice as an official selection of the 2002 Tokyo International Fantastic Film Festival before it was even put to celluloid. Not sure how that works . . . D: Tagawa. C: Mika Katsumura, Yoshiyuki Kubota, Daisuke Ryo, Ayumu Tokito. CREATIVE ACZA/FULL MEDIA/ GAGA/TRANSFORMER

O

OROCHI, THE EIGHT-HEADED DRAGON (J 1994, US 1994) *** Kind of flies under the radar of most daikaiju fans, but this captivating flick (rooted firmly in Japanese mythology) is well worth checking out. Seemingly born under a bad sign, Yamato Takeru (Masahiro Takashima) is nevertheless destined to become a "warrior of the gods." Well, at least the righteous gods. The evil deity Sukiomi, packed in ice and cruising through outer space, is preparing to thaw out and destroy Earth. A rambunctious showdown is inevitable. In the interim, there's plenty of slashing and severing (and timely ninja magic) as Yamato and his talented friends confront a devious sorcerer, a molten lava monster, a tentacled sea curiosity, and the flame-spewing Orochi – a King Ghidorah look-alike with extra heads. Directed by Takao Okawara with the same ingenuity (and budget) of his Heisei Era Godzilla outings, this tantalizing Toho one-off also features a fireball-flingin' warrior chick, an armored bird with impeccable timing, and a gigantic robo-samurai with superb swordsmanship. OROCHI is actually an update of the 1959 epic, NIPPON TANJU, released in the U.S. one year later as THE THREE TREASURES. The late, great Toshiro Mifune, as Yamato, battles an eight-headed marionette in that film, with Eiji Tsuburaya supervising the special effects. D: Okawara, C: Takashima, Yasuko Sawaguchi, Hiroshi Abe, Misashi Ishibashi, Hiroshi Fujioka. TOHO

P-Q

PARASITE EVE (J 1997, US 2001) **½ Mitochondria – the energy generators in cells – are a sly, malicious life form with a will of their own in this chilling adaptation of Hideaki Sena's best-selling novel. Gifted cell biologist Toshiaki Nagashima (Hiroshi Mikami) extracts the stuff from the liver of his his brain-dead wife, cultures the cells, and creates a clone of the missus – minus the nipples, for some reason. Regardless, Nagashima is still smitten as his spouse (portrayed by Riona Hazuki) is a fetching young thang. But it's soon obvious she's not quite right, morphing into a creeping ooze and expending mitochondrial energy to literally toast people. Apparently, the mitochondria plan on using human hosts to wipe out civilization! A promising rookie effort from director Maysuki Ochiai, who seamlessly weaves effective character development within a thought-provoking storyline. Incidentally, a popular PlayStation game also preceded this frightening flick. D: Ochiai. C: Mikami, Hazuki, Tomoko Nakajima, Ayaka Omura, Goro Inagaki, Hisako Manda, Tatsuya Bessho, Noboru Mitani. FUJI TELEVISION NETWORK/KADOKAWA SHOTEN

PRINCE OF SPACE (J 1959, US 1964) ** Look! Up in the sky! It's a bird . . . it's a plane . . . it's . . . the Prince of Space? Disguised as a mild-mannered shoeshine boy (specifically, a "bootblacker"), the affable and unassuming "Wally" slips into a white cape and tights to safeguard the globe from kooky alien invaders. Edited together from two full-length Japanese theatrical features, it's a fave among camp cinema fans, most likely due to the outlandish cackling of the movie's vile villain – the mustachioed, beak-nosed Ambassador Phantom of the Planet Krankor. Think Burgess Meredith as the Penguin but a couple of octaves lower. The Phantom and his minions kidnap Japan's finest scientific minds to aid in their fiendish plans of world takeover; that definitely isn't cool with the Prince. Good thing he's unaffected by their weapons, a fact he is wont to repeat again . . . and again . . . and again. Shot in spiffy black-and-white, PRINCE OF SPACE has the feel of a 1940s sci-fi serial, with wavering miniature spaceships and a plenitude of cosmic sound effects. A sight to behold: the goofy giant oaf who guards Krankor's home base. Topping it all off is a trio of school kids who seem light years smarter than the hopelessly befuddled grown-ups. D: Eijiro Wakabayashi. C: Tatsuo Umemiya, Joji Oka, Ushio Skashi, Hiroko Mine, Takashi Kanda. TOEI

PRINCESS BLADE, THE (J 2001, US 2002) **½ Remake of the 1973 slice-and-dice classic LADY SNOWBLOOD, but this time set in a futuristic, post-apocalyptic world rather than feudal Japan. Yuki, a 20-year-old, katana-carrying assassin, is the last remaining sovereign of a once-proud ruling class. Hired as part of a government-financed outfit to subdue insurgent forces, she discovers that her unit's leader was responsible for her mother's death 15 years earlier. Naturally, she seeks revenge. Played with reserve by actress/model Yumiko Shaku (GODZILLA AGAINST MECHAGODZILLA, SKY HIGH), Yuki is a tough little miss who takes a lickin' and keep on tickin'. There's a profusion of nimble acrobatics, supplemented with fast-paced, precisely-choreographed sword fights. Full-tilt fog machines and the use of blue lens filters give the pic a gloomy look. Real downer of an ending, too. But, you know, these tortured-soul sagas rarely conclude on a harmonious note. D: Shinsuke Sato. C: Shaku, Hideaki Ito, Shiro Sano, Yoichi Numata, Kiyusaka Shimada, Yoko Chosokabe. SHURAYUKIHIME FILM PARTNERS

PRINCESS FROM THE MOON (J 1987, US 1987) **½ Based on a centuries-old Japanese folktale, this fanciful flick features the esteemed Toshiro Mifune as a humble bamboo cutter who finds a newborn babe in the thick of a forest. But this is no ordinary tot. For one thing, the kid emerges from a cocoon. The lil' nipper also bears a remarkable resemblance to the bamboo cutter's recently-deceased daughter, but with haunting blue eyes. Undeterred, he takes the bundle of joy home to the wife. Believing she is heaven-sent, the couple decides to raise her as their own. The girl grows quickly into a young woman – literally, at an accelerated rate – and astounds with her ability to rapidly heal. Named Kaguya, we eventually learn she is an alien left stranded on Earth after her spacecraft crashed. The film's finale, with a majestic starship arriving to retrieve Kaguya, is reminiscent of CLOSE ENCOUNTERS OF THE THIRD KIND. A decent effort, certainly helped by Mifune's brooding presence. And it's directed by the renowned Kon Ichikawa. Megumi Odaka, later to play the psychic Miki Saegusa in the Heisei Era Godzilla movies, makes her screen debut as a sight-impaired lass. D: Ichikawa. C: Mifune, Ayaka Wakao, Yasuko Sawaguchi, Koji Ishizawa, Odaka. FUJI TELEVISION NETWORK/TOHO

PROPHECIES OF NOSTRADAMUS (J 1974, US 1979) ** Yowzers! Here's one wigged-out, weird disaster flick straight from that genre's peak in the mid-1970s. A scientist well-versed in the cataclysmic predictions of the 16th-century prophet Nostradamus, warns of the world's imminent demise – but to no avail. Sure enough, some awfully strange things occur. Radioactive smog creates mutated bats, killer plants, and enlarged, bloodsucking slugs. Rioting, traffic gridlock, and food shortages soon follow. The weather is, well, outright bizarre. Humankind, apathetic and irresponsible for decades, is now helpless. It's a bleak pic, for sure, that unapologetically sticks to its guns. Seldom seen nowadays – especially in Japan – as its depiction of nuclear radiation victims was considered offensive by a group representing atomic bomb survivors. Yoshimitsu Banno, director of the trippy GODZILLA VS. THE SMOG MONSTER, wrote a majority of the script. The U.S. version is 26 minutes shorter, sacrificing significant portions of carefully-constructed dialogue. FX fans: Hang tight 'til film's end, when Earth's unavoidable collapse is at the forefront. AKA: THE LAST DAYS OF PLANET EARTH, CATASTROPHE: 1999. D: Toshio Masuda. C: Tetsuro Tanba, Toshio Kurosawa, Kaoru Yumi, Yoko Tsukasa, So Yamamura. TOHO

R

REBIRTH OF MOTHRA (J 1996, US 1999) *** The starting point of the visually-striking Mothra trilogy of the 1990s finds the mondo moth battling old nemesis Desghidorah, a nasty sort awakened after 65 million years as a result of logging activities in the Hokkaido rain forest. Not a good thing, as the loathsome creature (a three-headed, fire-breathin', high-flyin' derivation of King Ghidorah) includes the obliteration of both life on Mars *and* Earth's dinosaurs on its resume. An aging but able Mothra unwaveringly appears with a dazzling array of attacks – antenna lasers, electric abdominal discharges, and sparkle dust emulsion – at her disposal. Of course, this being a Mothra movie and all, there's a couple of cutesy fairies to serenade us with their sweet song; riding high on a pint-sized version of Mothra, the diminutive dames reluctantly clash with evil sister Belvera (who dresses in black, utilizes a miniature dragon for transport, and terrorizes innocent children). A rare male variant of Mothra also emerges, hatching from its egg on Infant Island and eventually transforming from dull-colored caterpillar to brightly-mottled moth. Be forewarned: This pic includes one of the most gut-wrenching scenes in daikaiju history. Kiddos may prefer the more lighthearted REBIRTH OF MOTHRA II. D: Okihiko Yoneda. C: Megumi Kobayashi, Sayaka Yamaguchi, Aki Hano, Kazuki Futami. TOHO

REBIRTH OF MOTHRA II (J 1997, US 2000) **** The middle installment of the vibrant Mothra triad of films from the Heisei Era is beautifully paced, funny, and indisputably one of the more entertaining Japanese monster flicks for the preadolescent crowd. Three fresh-faced youths (clever girl, hefty sumo kid, and nerdy boy) journey to the fabled underwater kingdom of Nilai-Kanai in search of a mysterious treasure. Along the way they come across an odd lot of characters – large and small – like the legendary Ghogo, a white furball whose urine has magical healing powers. Returning from REBIRTH OF MOTHRA are the colorfully-clad Elias, the two tiny fairies from

Mothra's home, Infant Island. (The lovely ladies, by the way, do a bang-up job on Mothra's time-honored theme song.) The twins' bad-in-black sis Belvera is also back, as sassy as ever. Mothra glides in to preserve the planet when the ancient sea denizen Dagahra surfaces due to Japan's rising pollution levels. The mighty moth can now morph into a slick, subaquatic configuration known as Aqua Mothra; Koichi Kawakita's creative special effects work seems to know no bounds. Director Kunio Miyoshi's first daikaiju eiga is an overlooked masterpiece. D: Miyoshi. C: Megumi Kobayashi, Sakaya Yamaguchi, Aki Hano, Hikari Mitsushima. TOHO

REBIRTH OF MOTHRA III (J 1998, US 2003) *** King Ghidorah, the dastardly bad boy of daikaiju cinema, is at it again. This time the triple-headed titan is kidnapping Japanese schoolchildren by sucking 'em up into mid-air and teleporting 'em to a huge, pliable dome. Mothra, the magnificent giant moth, comes to the rescue; the bold yet sensible insect gets one look at the belligerant King G and decides it's better to shift into "light speed" mode, travel back 130 million years to prehistoric times, and take on a younger, less-daunting Ghidorah before it has a chance to mature. Meanwhile, unanticipated support is provided when fashionable fairies Moll and Lora (Mothra's gal pals from Infant Island) reconcile with black sheep sister Belvera. The last film of the highly-imaginative Heisei trilogy, a concerted effort is again made to connect with pre-teen viewers. Mothra's newfound capacity to convert into armored form is something to see. D: Okihiro Yoneda. C: Megumi Kobayashi, Misato Tate, Aki Hano, Atsushi Onita, Koichi Ueda. TOHO

RETURN OF DAIMAJIN See RETURN OF THE GIANT MAJIN

RETURN OF MAJIN See RETURN OF THE GIANT MAJIN

RETURN OF THE GIANT MAJIN (J 1966, US 1968) **½ The big stone dude with the attitude is back! Majin, the colossal statue that comes to life, reappears in the second of a three-film series to save serfs in olden Japan from an evil conqueror's reign of terror. Like its forerunner, MAJIN, MONSTER OF TERROR, we wait until the final reel for the granite-gray "rock god" to wake up and do some serious stompin'. In the meantime, the first hour of the flick teems with swordplay and slaughter but, unbelievably, no blood! Majin is seen in this entry as a deity by the villagers, rather than a rampant spirit. Nice special effects moment: Blasted to bits and pieces by the baddies, Majin rises – fully intact – from the depths of a lake and parts the water like Heston in DeMille's TEN COMMANDMENTS. Wow! MAJIN STRIKES AGAIN would follow. AKA: RETURN OF DAIMAJIN, RETURN OF MAJIN, WRATH OF DAIMAJIN. D: Kenji Misumi. C: Kojiro Hongo, Shiho Fujimura, Taro Marui, Jutaro Hojo, Takashi Kanda. DAIEI

RETURN OF THE GIANT MONSTERS (J 1967, US 1967) *** Gamera's third film, and by now the mega-sized flying turtle is a full-fledged protector of Earth. Our lava-loving friend has his claws full with the vicious Gyaos, a bloodthirsty prehistoric bird with some darn-nifty scrappin' abilities. Gyaos emits a yellowish smoke from its belly that extinguishes fires; razor-sharp laser beams from the creature's squawker slice planes (and a random car) clean in half. Sure, things would get noticeably nuttier in the series' next outing (DESTROY ALL PLANETS) but this one definitely has its moments. Example: A famished Gyaos is lured to a massive turntable by a large vat of synthetic blood. Scientists flip the switch and the crazed kaiju is soon spinning at a frenzied pace! Will the inexorable Gyaos be too dizzy to go on? Another sign of what was to come: A chubby-cheeked lad named Eichi is rescued by Gamera and gets the ride of his life aboard his big-hearted buddy. AKA: GAMERA VS. GAOS, GAMERA VS. GYAOS. D: Noriaka Yuasa. C: Kojiro Hongo, Naoyuki Abe, Kichijiro Ueda, Reiko Kasahara. DAIEI

RETURNER (J 2002, US 2003) ***½ Uptempo, stylish flick about a female soldier sent, via time travel, to present-day Japan to halt the annihilation of mankind in 2084 by riled-up extraterrestrials. Our heroine, adorable yet tough as nails, enlists the aid of a hip, highly-efficient hit man with an awful big chip on his shoulder. The duo learns that a ruthless crime boss is in possession of a recently-crashed spaceship and has abducted its otherworldly pilot. Decades of needless warfare can be averted by simply returning the interplanetary creature to its people. The bad guys, however, ain't buyin' it. For sure, movies contemplating the space-time continuum tend to leave questions unanswered but it's easy to get lost in this film's thrilling, uninhibited action. The CGI visual work is stunning; the reconfiguration of a big ol' jet airliner into a complex alien mothership is a substantial feat. Director Takashi Yamazaki also handled the effects and co-wrote the script. A sequel is rumored to be in the development stages.

D: Yamazaki. C: Takeshi Kaneshiro, Anne Suzuki, Kirin Kiki. AMUSE/FUJI TELEVISION NETWORK/IMAGICA/ ROBOT COMMUNICATIONS/SHIROGAMI/TOHO

ROBOGEISHA (J 2009, US 2009) ** Geisha girls – long an embodiment of elegance and grace in Japanese culture – are given a mechanical makeover in Noboru Iguchi's absurd take on sibling conflict. Fans of Iguchi's films (MACHINE GIRL is the most familiar) are drawn to the director's unfiltered weirdness. The cyborg geishas in this feverish flick are furnished with way-out embellishments, such as machine gun boobage and protracting butt blades! Yoshie Kasuga, a woeful young missy, and older sister Kikue – a well-known geisha – are captured by a clandestine faction and turned into lethal assassins. Ninja stars, knives, buzzsaws, etc. astonishingly emerge from every conceivable orifice. The gals defy their captors, and despite a caustic love-hate relationship, mend fences in an effort to prevent a giant robot castle from walking right up and dropping a freakin' nuclear bomb into Mt. Fuji. Yep, this is over-the-top stuff, augmented with liberal doses of gore and spatter – an Iguchi staple. If your idea of cinematic merriment is watching folks get their faces blistered from boiling hot spurts of breast milk, then ROBOGEISHA is your movie. The 2010 DVD release by FUNimation includes a 17-minute Iguchi-helmed offshoot, GEISHA COP: FEARSOME GEISHA COPS – GO TO HELL. D: Iguchi. C: Aya Kiguchi, Hitomi Hasabe, Takumi Saito, Etsuka Ikuta, Taro Shigaki. KADOKAWA/MOVIE GATE/ PONY CANYON/T.O. ENTERTAINMENT

ROBOMAN HAKAIDER See MECHANICAL VIOLATOR HAIKAIDER

RODAN (J 1956, US 1957) **½ Yikes! A terrifying pair of agile, fast-flying pteranodons have ascended from the crusty substructure of Earth to cause a worldwide "flap." Soaring at supersonic speeds, the relentless birds bring forth hurricane-force wind gusts as buildings disintegrate, vehicles are swept asunder, and debris is wildly scattered. The resourceful Eiji Tsuburaya does a marvelous job, as usual, with the special effects. Our story begins with a number of gruesome, unexplained deaths in a rustic mining settlement. The culprits are discovered to be 10-foot-long insect critters that inhabit the deepest of the mines. The ravenous Rodan find these creepy-crawlies to be a mouthwatering treat, so they're staying put. The Japanese army is brought in to launch their customary barrage of artillery. Will military might make right? Notable for being the first Toho science-fiction film in color. D: Ishiro Honda. C: Kenji Sahara, Yumi Shirakawa, Akihiko Hirata, Akio Kobori. TOHO

S

SAMURAI PRINCESS (J 2009, US 2009) *½ This one's another of the sci-fi splatterfests that have been popping up in Japan in recent years. You can expect the usual: disjoined body parts, gushing blood, and gore galore. Adult video actress Aino Kishi stars as an android ninja in pursuit of the deranged mutants that raped and killed 11 of her friends. Our fearless protagonist is equipped with atypical weaponry, including a chest chainsaw and – get this – bosom grenades! Kishi's soft-core sex scene pretty much seals the deal that this pic is not for the kids. Ultimately, as is the case with these sorta flicks, story takes a backseat to the unceasing torrent of blood and guts. All of the effects work and makeup was done by Yoshihiro Nishimura, the guy who directed TOKYO GORE POLICE. Catch that film first, or MEATBALL MACHINE, if you're interested in bigger-budgeted representations of this burgeoning genre. D: Kenjo Kaji. C: Kishi, Asuka Kataoka, Mao Shina, Mitsuru Karahashi, Dai Mizuno, Noriko Kajima, Miki Harase. SAMURAI PRINCESS PRODUCTION COMMITTEE

SAYONARA JUPITER (J 1984, US 2007) ** Seven years in the planning, this outer space epic was a critical disappointment in Japan despite its lofty ambitions. Favoring drama over action, it's nonetheless a platform for Koichi Kawakita's budding special effects skills. It's the early 22nd century, and the United Earth Federation hopes to transform Jupiter into a second sun. Neighboring planets would then become habitable, and Earth would be supplied with additional solar energy. But, as fate would have it, a friggin' black hole is approaching. Blasting Jupiter into oblivion can alter its course, but radical protesters (led by the hippie-dippy singer/songwriter/guitarist "Peter") oppose the project and do their best to muck it up. Sounds intriguing but beware: This flick isn't in a hurry to go anywhere fast. Special attention is lavished on the elaborate miniatures, with the camera slowly panning to capture the intricacies of an eclectic assortment of spacecraft. Check out the imposing Jupiter Ghost, an alien vessel (or is it a life form?) hovering amidst our title planet's gaseous atmosphere. There's also a (in what I'm surmising may be a cinematic first) zero-gravity sexual tryst. Based on the book by the acclaimed Japanese novelist Sakyo Komatsu, who also co-directed. D: Koji Hashimoto, Komatsu. C: Tomokazu Miura, Diane Dangely, Akihiko Hirata, Miyuki Ono. TOHO

SECRET OF THE TELEGIAN, THE (J 1960, US 1961) **½ Do not attempt to adjust the picture. The strange, luminous fellow you see before you is actually a human television transmission, crackling with static, and bent on revenge. Callously left for dead by his platoon 15 years earlier, war vet Goro (Tadao Nakamura) reemerges with the ability to teleport himself across electrical lines and straight into the homes of those who wronged him! The police are perplexed – and powerless to stop the elusive Goro's homicidal binge. A deft mix of mystery, sci-fi, and crime noir from director Jun Fukuda, who would later helm five Showa Era Godzilla flicks. Not sure why, but the U.S. version was released in black-and-white. The film fares much better in its original retro color (***) as Goro's fluctuating bluish hue is of constant visual interest. D: Fukuda. C: Koji Tsuruta, Yumi Shirakawa, Nakamura, Yoshio Tsuchiya, Akihiko Hirata. TOHO

SHIN GODZILLA (J 2016, US 2016) *** Many expected Toho's first Godzilla movie since 2004 to be an antithesis to the American depictions of the famed creature. TriStar's 1998 endeavor basically featured a rather ordinary giant iguana, and the 2012 Legendary release – though faithful in its rendering of the big guy – drew mixed reviews from fans in the know. SHIN GODZILLA, however, is not a reaction to the U.S. films but an allegory regarding the bureaucratic red tape hindering the relief efforts following the 2011 Tohoku earthquake and tsunami, and the ensuing Fukushima Daichi nuclear disaster. The pic is ladened with dialogue, but it definitely struck a chord with Japanese audiences. Western viewers bemoaned "not enough Godzilla!" and for good reason; the scenes involving the reprehensible reptile are simply beyond belief. Godzilla is a sheer force of evil gone bonkers. His atomic breath is crazy powerful and often uncontrollable. The damage done is devastating. And geez, it's the ugliest Godzilla we've seen to date, with sunken eyes, uneven teeth, open sores, and exposed muscle tissue. His presentation, enhanced by CGI, was achieved by filming an actor in a motion-capture suit. The 29th Godzilla outing by Toho and the franchise's first true reboot; no mention is made of any pre-existing Godzilla. Hideaki Anno and Shinji Higuchi co-directed, with Anno authoring the script and Higuchi managing the VFX. Shin, incidentally, means "true," "new," or "god" in Japanese. AKA: GODZILLA: RESURGENCE. D: Anno, Higuchi. C: Hiroki Hasegawa, Yutaka Takenouchi, Satomi Ishihara, Shinya Tsukamoto, Kora Kengo. TOHO/CINE BAZAR/FUNIMATION

SIX ULTRA BROTHERS VS. THE MONSTER ARMY, THE See SPACE WARRIORS 2000

SON OF GODZILLA (J 1967, US 1968) *** One might describe the hardheaded Godzilla's parenting style as "tough love" but can you blame him? From the moment his roly-poly offspring hatches from his shell in this "coming of age"

flick, the kid is, quite frankly, soft. Maybe dragging the little guy by the hindquarters is a tad harsh. But with three gigantic praying mantises (aptly dubbed "Gimantises") and an enormous web-spitting spider named Spiga seeking a hearty meal, junior needs to grow a pair – and quick. The hullabaloo takes place on a remote South Seas island, where a team of sweaty research scientists are conducting wacky weather experiments. Despite scorching half of the island, the capable Toho cast is nevertheless likeable. Akira Kubo stands out (as always) as a tireless reporter who drops in on the proceedings by way of parachute. This engaging pic also includes what is perhaps the most talked-about scene in the annals of daikaiju eiga filmdom. Big Daddy G teaches his apprehensive son, known as "Minya" in the U.S., the finer points of radioactive breath-blasting. Minya wheezes a few meager smoke rings until Papa stamps on the impressionable tyke's tail to get the desired effect. Comical father-and-son consultations are interspersed throughout, and are sure to appeal to the youngest viewers. D: Jun Fukuda. C: Tadao Takashima, Kubo, Bibari Maeda, Akihiko Hirata, Kenji Sahara, Yoshio Tsuchiya. TOHO

SPACE AMOEBA See YOG, MONSTER FROM SPACE

SPACE BATTLESHIP YAMATO (J 2010, US 2012) ***1/2 Things are looking rather dismal for Mother Earth in the year 2199. The populace has gone underground after a horde of heinous aliens – the Gamilas – went and pelted the planet with radioactive meteorite bombs. And it looks like they're playing for keeps. The opening credits have barely rolled and we're thrust into the teeth of a rousing outer space encounter between our film's courageous fighter pilots and the interstellar evildoers. Total annihilation is inevitable when, lo and behold, an urgent message arrives from the planet Iscandar. Apparently, these cosmic cats possess a device that removes radiation from the ozone. Seems swell, so Japanese officials fetch, of all things, the storied World War II battleship Yamato from the bottom of the sea. Sunk in 1944, the big boat is in obvious need of refurbishment. A supercharged propulsion system is incorporated, giving the ship the power of flight, ultrapotent munitions, and (gasp!) warping capabilities. A brash, young captain (screen idol Takuya Kimura) and a down-to-business navigator (Meisa Kuroki of ASSAULT GIRLS) lead the Yamato's able crew on an astral adventure to save our planet. Hopes were high for this flick, as it's adapted from a landmark 1970s anime of the same name. (It later showed up in the States as STAR BLAZERS.) Director Takashi Yamazaki certainly had the cachet to pull it off, having made both the sci-fi actioner RETURNER, and the widely-praised ALWAYS: SUNSET ON THIRD STREET. Yamazaki also spearheads YAMATO's CGI-heavy special effects, putting the viewer plumb in the middle of several STAR WARS-type space chases. That's the movie's main draw but it's all balanced out by an effective, sustainable narrative. D: Yamazaki. C: Kimura, Kuroki, Toshiro Yanagiba, Naoto Ogata, Maiko. TOKYO BROADCASTING SYSTEM/SEDIC INTERNATIONAL/ROBOT COMMUNICATIONS

SPACE MONSTER GAMERA See GAMERA: SUPER MONSTER

SPACE NINJA: SWORD OF THE SPACE ARK See SWORDS OF THE SPACE ARK

SPACE WARRIORS 2000 (THAI 1974, J 1979, US 1985) *½ Hands down, one of the craziest flicks you'll ever see. In fact, I'm not sure what the heck was going on here. Was I suffering from a blow to the head I couldn't recall? Side effects from a new med? Naw – the film is just flat-out wacked. Hardcore Ultraman fans may wince at this Japanese-Thai co-production, comprised of a mish-mash of scenes pulled directly from various television episodes and motion pictures of the long-revered tokusatsu franchise. Ultraman, and five of his flippin,' cartwheelin' Ultra colleagues, team up with the giant, prancing monkey-god Hanuman to battle five squealing, rubbery-blubbery monstrosities. The skirmishes, at times, resemble an out-of-control gymnastics class. Somewhere along the line, Tsuburaya Productions sued the Thai production company, claiming the eventual final version was compiled without their approval. As it is, this one is good for some unexpected deep-from-the-gut guffaws. AKA: THE SIX ULTRA BROTHERS VS. THE MONSTER ARMY, SPACE WARRIORS 2000: THE YEAR OF THE MONKEY WRENCH. D: Sompote Sands, Dick Randall, Marc Smith, Shohei Toji. C: Ko Kaeoduendee, Anan Prichan, Yodchay Mekusan, Smith. CHAIYO PRODUCTIONS/FUJI EIGA/TSUBURAYA PRODUCTIONS

SPACE WARRIORS 2000: THE YEAR OF THE MONKEY WRENCH See SPACE WARRIORS 2000

STAR FORCE: FUJITIVE ALIEN II (J 1978, US 1986) *½ Star Wolf Ken, Captain Joe, and the rest of the intrepid crew of the Bacchus-3 return for more space-age lunacy in this outlandish sequel to FUJITIVE ALIEN. This time, the gang travels to a far-off planet to destroy an evil alien race's doomsday weapon. Other than that, the plot is sorta freeform. There's trouble, however, at every turn. And although he has tempered his fondness for the hooch, Captain Joe remains the kind of guy who flies by the seat of his pants. Spliced together from episodes of a Japanese television program, there's quite a bit of aimless action. It's an easy flick to goof on, but for many that's part of the fun. D: Minoru Kanaya. C: Tatsuma Azuma, Miyuki Tanigawa, Jo Shishido, Choei Takahashi, Tsutomu Yukawa, Hiro Tateyama. TSUBURAYA PRODUCTIONS

SUPER MONSTER See GAMERA: SUPER MONSTER

SWORDS OF THE SPACE ARK (J 1979, US 1981) *½ Pared down to a feature-length release from a Japanese television series, SWORDS is regarded as the sequel to the wild and zany MESSAGE FROM SPACE. Though it's similarly zippy and colorful, the connection is tenuous at best. When an intergalactic baddie and his flunkies take over a defenseless planet, a brave trio of outer space itinerants jump into action. (Our loquacious pilot is the scene-stealing Baru, a cigar-smoking apeman.) Crammed into this caffeinated film's 70 minutes are numerous katana clashes, a torrent of laser fire, and good ol'-fashioned hand-to-hand combat. A floating sea vessel, ghostly-white masts fully hoisted, is the prime link to this pic's predecessor. Also traversing the outer reaches is a massive spacecraft disguised as a Majin-like stone totem. It all looks good on paper but be prepared: This is clearly the work of maniacal minds. AKA: MESSAGE FROM OUTER SPACE, SPACE

NINJA: SWORD OF THE SPACE ARK. D: Minoru Yamada, Bunker Jenkins. C: Hiroyuki Sanada, Akira Odo, Ryo Nishida, Yoko Akitani. TOEI

T

TERROR BENEATH THE SEA (J 1966, US 1971) *½ Strictly for B-movie enthusiasts. Shinichi "Sonny" Chiba (the STREETFIGHTER films) and Peggy Neal (THE X FROM OUTER SPACE) are reporters covering the Navy's testing of a new, high-tech homing torpedo; they inadvertently come upon a secret underwater base, where a madman in dark shades is turning innocent folk into harpoon-shooting, amphibious slaves. His intent, not surprisingly, is to rule the world. Some serious butt-kicking is in order, and Chiba (later a star of action pics) obliges – albeit at film's end. The flick's gill creatures (actors in loose-fitting, wrinkly costumes) are quite the sight. Those who flip over this sort of stuff will get a charge out of 'em. Director Hajime Sato also guided the underrated GOKE, BODYSNATCHER FROM HELL. D: Sato. C: Chiba, Neal, Eric Nielsen, Franz Gruber, Andrew Hughes. TOEI/FUJITA ASSOCIATES/RAM

TERROR OF GODZILLA, THE See TERROR OF MECHAGODZILLA

TERROR OF MECHAGODZILLA (J 1975, US 1978) **½ Somewhat of a detour from the upbeat, kid-friendly Godzilla fare of the 1970s, TERROR OF MECHAGODZILLA is nonetheless effectively gloomy. Insufferable aliens from the Third Planet of the Black Hole (huh?) reinvent Mechagodzilla, the 400-foot-high robot double of Godzilla. The plan? Demolish the world and rebuild it more to their liking. Thanks to a disillusioned scientist and his cyborg daughter, the extraterrestrial scoundrels have access to a monstrous bipedal sea horse named Titanosaurus. The Big G, in his now-familiar role as Earth's protector, is up for the challenge. This noble effort unfortunately flopped at the box office despite the return of two legendary figures to the Godzilla fold. Ishiro Honda was back to direct his first picture with the notorious lizard since 1969's GODZILLA'S REVENGE, though it would be the final (and 47th) film he would helm in his illustrious career. Also featured was Akira Ifukube's first original music score since 1968's DESTROY ALL MONSTERS. Godzilla movies, for the time being, had run their course, and we wouldn't see "ol' atomic breath" again until GODZILLA 1985. AKA: THE TERROR OF GODZILLA. D: Honda. C: Katsuhiko Sasaki, Tomoko Ai, Akihiko Hirata, Katsumasa Uchida, Goro Mutsumi. TOHO

TETSUJIN 28 (J 2005, US 2006) **½ Live-action adaptation of the classic anime series best known to American audiences as GIGANTOR. Shotaro Kaneda, a vociferous 12-year-old, discovers that his late father, a distinguished scientist, developed a giant, remote-controlled robot – Tetsujin 28 – to be hailed during times of crisis. When the vengeful terrorist Zero attacks Japan with his own big bot – the imposing Black Ox – an ill-equipped Shotaro is the only option to operate our metallic title character, which is tucked away in mothballs at his dad's secluded island lab. The titanic twosome (computer-generated, by the way) duke it out in the streets of midtown Tokyo. The use of CGI actually helps this flick stay true to its roots, as our rock 'em, sock 'em combatants retain an animated look. Harmless fun, but definitely geared toward the kiddos. D: Shin Togashi. C: Sosuke Ikematsu, Yu Aoi, Hiroko Yakushimaru, Teruyuki Kagawa. SHOCHIKU

TETSUO: THE IRON MAN (J 1989, US 1992) ** Not for the faint of heart. Bizarre, frightening tale of a Japanese salaryman who mutates into an odd conglomeration of metal components, cables, tubes, and wires; furthermore, he's endowed with a whirring phallic drill. Needless to say, it's also not for the young ones. As our tortured main character painfully transmogrifies into a walking scrap heap, we're subjected to a nightmare world of gore, violence, and perversity. Is it real or imagined? Shinya Tsukamoto gained notice by directing, writing, and editing this hyperkinetic cult classic, and he plays a key role in the picture as a metal fetishist. It's not everyone's cup of tea, but there's a keen appreciation in certain circles. Often compared to the works of David Cronenberg and David Lynch, but weirder. Filmed in 16mm black-and-white, it clocks out at a brisk 67 minutes. The higher-budgeted TETSUO II: BODY HAMMER would come next. D: Tsukamoto. C: Tomorowo Taguchi, Kei Fujiwara, Nobu Kanaoka, Tsukamoto. KAIJYU THEATER

TETSUO II: BODY HAMMER (J 1992, US 1997) ** Shinya Tsukamoto's frenetic follow-up to his cyberpunk benchmark TETSUO: THE IRON MAN is just as jarring and horrific as its prototype. Like it or not, it's a visual undertaking you won't soon forget. Tomorowo Taguchi returns as the bespectacled businessman who morphs into a half-man, half-metal meld when pushed to the brink. Tsukamoto pulls double duty; in addition to directing, he plays the unstable leader of a gang of psycho mutants. His drastic experiments accelerate Tetsuo's gruesome conversion to a guns a-blazin' killing machine. Lensed in dim colors, Tsukamoto's Tokyo has an industrial, gritty feel. Tough to get next to for a lot of folks but this is the work of a filmmaker with a unique vision. D: Tsukamoto. C: Taguchi, Nobu Kanaoka, Tsukamoto, Sujin Kim. KAIJYU THEATER/TOSHIBA EMI

TETSUO: THE BULLET MAN (J 2010, US 2010) **½ Perhaps to appeal to a broader fan base, this third – and latest – of director Shinya Tsukamoto's unsettling Tetsuo flicks was made with an English-speaking cast. The premise, however, remains the same. An ordinary fellow (played here by Eric Bossick) is jolted by a life-altering experience and shortly thereafter transforms into a murderous, metallic mutant. This entry even provides a plausible explanation for our lead character's agonizing metamorphosis. Combine intense rage with the DNA inherited from an android mother and the result is a bullet-spraying, revenge-minded creature of mass destruction. Interestingly, this pic was showcased at several film fests around the world in 2009 before its 2010 Japanese release. Tsukamoto was thrilled when industrial rockers Nine Inch Nails agreed to compose the movie's closing theme. D: Tsukamoto. C: Bossick, Akiko Mono, Yuko Nakimura, Stephen Sarrazin, Tsukamoto, Tiger Charlie Gerhardt,Prakhar Jain. KAIJYU THEATER/ASMIK ACE ENTERTAINMENT/YAHOO JAPAN

TIDAL WAVE (J 1973, US 1975) ** Known as SUBMERSION OF JAPAN in its native land, where it made big bucks at the box office. The heavily-edited American release (over half of the original film's 143 minutes are dumped) tacks on scenes of BONANZA star Lorne Greene – as the U.S. prez – reacting to a series of natural disasters ravaging Japan. Fortunately, Teruyoshi Nakano's superb SFX work is left untouched. Rumblings beneath the surface result in earthquakes, floods, volcanic discharge, fires, and ultimately, a devastating tsunami. There's little recourse as the island nation sinks into a watery abyss. Based on the novel by the noted sci-fi author, Sakyo Komatsu; the flick was redone in 2006 with Shinji Higuchi, the special effects wiz of the 1990s Gamera trilogy, as the director. D: Shiro Moritami, Andrew Meyer. C: Greene, Keiju Kobayashi, Hiroshi Fujioka, Ayumi Ishida, Tatsuro Tanba. TOHO

TIME OF THE APES (J 1974, US 1987) *½ Sort of the Far East answer to PLANET OF THE APES. It's yet another offering from American film distributor Sandy Frank where episodes of a Japanese TV series (this time, THE APE CORPS) are re-edited to create a full-length feature. Seeking cover in cryogenic capsules when an earthquake strikes, a young woman and two children are unintentionally catapulted through time to a world inhabited by militaristic apes. They chance upon a sole human, Godo, a warrior dude living in the jungle who is feared by the simians. A succession of harrowing chases follow. Oddly, the big bad primates use rotary telephones and drive 1970s-era luxury cars. Also, for no discernible reason, a flying saucer darts in every now and then to photograph the commotion. Hmm. D: Kiyasumi Fukuzawa, Atsuo Okunawa. C: Reiko

Tokunaga, Hiroko Saito, Masaaki Kaji, Tetsuya Ushida. TSUBURAYA PRODUCTIONS

TIME SLIP (J 1979, US 1981) *** Sonny Chiba and a squad of modern-day soldiers are unexpectedly hurtled back in time to the chaos of feudal Japan in this bracing adventure from unsung director Kosei Saito. Simultaneously caught in the time warp: a helicopter, tank, patrol boat, and a couple of heavy-duty transport rigs. Real handy-dandy, as an arrow-slingin' primitive army, vast in numbers, is on the attack. Chiba, playing the unit's head honcho, has ample opportunity to show off his finely-honed fighting skills. He also surmises that the platoon's only way to return to their own time is to gain rule of Japan, thereby changing history. Good luck with that one. The enemy is annoyingly persistent. And how are they gonna refuel those fancy-schmancy combat vehicles in the 16th century? Undaunted, the undermanned grunts join forces with a strident band of samurai to form an interesting, if unlikely, alliance. Distracting are the syrupy pop ballads that crop up at inopportune moments throughout the pic. Even so, this is an appealing, action-filled watch. AKA: G.I. SAMURAI. D: Saito. C: Chiba, Isao Natsuyagi, Tsunehiko Watase, Koji Naki. KADOKAWA

TIME TRAVELLER: THE GIRL WHO LEAPT THROUGH TIME (J 2010, US 2011) *** Here's a charming – and dare I say it – romantic sci-fi drama that, gosh darn it, tugs at the ol' heartstrings. Kazuko Yoshiyama, a brilliant chemist who has concocted a time-travel serum, is injured in an automobile mishap. She briefly emerges from a coma to send her daughter Akari, a college-bound schoolgirl, back to an earlier era to deliver an important message to an individual identified as Kazuo Fukamachi. Akari (Riisa Naka) is adorable but a little ditzy. Instead of drifting back to 1972 Tokyo, she errs and winds up in the year 1974. Unable to find any trace of the elusive Kazuo, she secures the help of the younger personage of her mother and a fledgling moviemaker named Ryota. Akari begins to really dig Ryota, making an already muddled situation a lot more complicated. Derived from the novel by Yasutaka Tsutsui, this endearing tale has spurred numerous big-screen interpretations, including a well-received 2006 animated version. Director Masaaki Taniguchi, in his first feature, draws out nuanced performances from a competent cast. The film's gentle flow is downright intoxicating. D: Taniguchi. C: Naka, Kinobu Nakao, Narumi Yasuda, Masanobu Katsumora. ANIPLEX/EPIC RECORDS/STYLE JAM/VOICE AND HEART

TOKYO BLACKOUT (J 1987, US 1987) ** Lights out, folks! TOKYO BLACKOUT is yet another flick inspired by a book from the prolific Sakyo Komatsu, the guy who penned "Sayonara Jupiter," "The Submersion of Japan," and "Virus." An eerie electromagnetic cloud envelops Tokyo, isolating its 12 million residents from the outside world. It's up to a brave team of scientists and reporters to penetrate the volatile fog and solve the dilemma. But it's no walk in the park, as the mysterious mass has a tendency to spit out thunderbolts at those who venture near. Meanwhile, the U.S. and the Soviets show up and flex their muscles. Great idea for a movie, but this one's long on dialogue. Decent special effects, though. Lotsa' luck finding it, too, as the film had a limited run in the States. D: Toshio Masuda. C:

Tsunehiko Watase, Yuko Natori, Shinji Yamashita, Yoko Ishino. DAIEI

TOKYO GORE POLICE (J 2008, US 2008) **½ I'm guessing that some sorta record was set in this twisted flick for the sheer amount of fake blood splashed across the screen. (And yes, I've seen DEAD ALIVE.) The vital fluids flow freely, even from an unlucky gent's dismembered member. Seems that an unhinged scientist has created a virus that turns human beings into grotesque creatures. And you know what else? The friggin' things sprout unusual weaponry from open wounds! Enter the blade-brandishing Ruka, a female police officer who's quite proficient at carving these macabre malformations into tiny pieces. The hacking and hewing is relentless; one sorry fellow gets his legs chopped off but utilizes the rapid gush of blood as jet propulsion! Some strange stuff goes down, for sure. Amazingly, director Yoshihiro Nishimura shot and finished the film in just two weeks. D: Nishimura. C: Eihi Shina, Itsuji Itao, Yukahide Benny, Ji Ji Bu, Ikuko Sawada. NIKKATSU/FEVER DREAMS

TOKYO: THE LAST MEGALOPOLIS (J 1988, US 1993) ** Must admit I should have taken better notes while watching this mind-numbing flick. It's an ambitious pic that covers a heckuva lot of ground. People come and go, and it all seems so . . . confusing. But here goes. It's post World War I Japan, and a progress-oriented group plans on constructing earthquake-proof buildings in Tokyo. This bold proposal incenses the evil psychic sorcerer Kato, who wishes to level the city and return it to its former holy state. Garbed in military uniform, the malevolent Kato (Kyusaku

Shimada) summons a cadre of sinister spirits to conspire in his dirty deeds. Unfazed, muny officials devise an ingenious underground subway system, its formation bolstered by the golden, steam-powered robot, Gakutensoku. Kato and his ethereal allies promptly smash the thing to bits. Called upon to prevent the onslaught are spirits of a positive nature, most prominently a tenacious female warrior named Keiko. Stylishly rendered in subdued hues by cinematographer Masao Nakabori; the "cutting edge" goho doji infiltrating Tokyo by night were designed by H.R. Giger of ALIEN fame. Followed by a pair of sequels yet to see U.S. release. D: Akio Jissoji. C: Shintaro Katsu, Shimada, Mieko Harada, Junichi Ishida. EXE

20TH CENTURY BOYS 1: BEGINNING OF THE END (J 2008, US 2009) **** A major box-office hit in Japan, this tour-de-force adaptation of Naoki Urasawa's popular manga was produced on a budget of six billion yen, an extravagant expenditure for that country's motion picture industry. But you know what? It's the likeable characters and engrossing storyline that'll really hook ya. We learn that back in 1969, Kenji Endo and his boyhood companions gathered in their grassy hideout and wrote "The Book of Prophecies," a far-fetched account of a diabolical organization plotting global takeover by way of induced plagues, covert attacks, and a rampaging giant robot. Fast forward to the year 2000. Incredibly, the events detailed in "The Book of Prophecies" actually start to unfold. Kenji, now the unobtrusive manager of a convenient store, reunites with his old pals to get to the bottom of it all. An enigmatic cult leader named Friend is the likely culprit. Things get ugly fast when Friend dispatches the aforementioned automaton to spray a blood-draining liquid amongst the masses. Can Kenji and his crew save the world? The film's title is taken from the T-Rex song, "20th Century Boy," a favorite of former rocker Kenji. Two sequels – just as riveting – would follow. D: Yukihiko Tsutsumi. C: Toshiaki Karasawa, Etsushi Toyokawa, Takako Tokiwa, Teruyuki Kagawa, Hidehiko Ishizuka, Takashi Ukaji. 20TH CENTURY BOYS FILM PARTNERS

20TH CENTURY BOYS 2: THE LAST HOPE (J 2009, US 2009) *** It's 2015 – a scant 15 years after Earth's entire population was nearly exposed to a nasty germ unleashed by the evil cult leader known as Friend. But get this: Friend is now worshipped as a compassionate potentate, and the Secret Base Gang – saviors of the world – are blamed for the ghastly assault. The sequel to 2008's 20TH CENTURY BOYS: BEGINNING OF THE END can be somewhat taxing for the uninitiated but it's certainly an entertaining watch. When the pretentious Friend starts to fancy himself a god, the imperturbable Kenji Endo (Toshiaki Karasawa) and the rest of his Secret Base Gang cohorts come out of hiding. They're assisted by Kenji's defiant niece Kanna, who has little patience for Friend's revisionist history. Pay close attention as this sci-fi/mystery cleverly unfolds. 20TH CENTURY BOYS III: REDEMPTION would complete the trilogy later in the year. D: Yukihiko Tsutsumi. C: Karasawa, Etsushi Toyokawa, Takako Tokiwa, Airi Taira, Teruyuki Tagawa, Haruka Kinami. 20TH CENTURY BOYS FILM PARTNERS

20TH CENTURY BOYS 3: REDEMPTION (J 2009, US 2009) ***½ This compelling conclusion of the highly-regarded 20TH CENTURY BOYS ternion finds Japan, along with the rest of the world, still mesmerized by the dapper, masked cult leader referred to as "Friend." In fact, he's looked upon by some as a deity for his reputed ability to foresee future catastrophes. Kenji Endo, and his tight-knit posse, know better. After all, it's their fantastic sci-fi stories, conceived almost 50 years earlier, which are implausibly playing out before their very eyes. (This "Friend" was apparently a youthful acquaintance. But who is he?) Unbeknownst to the general public, the seemingly altruistic Friend is intent on abolishing mankind. He predicts an upcoming alien invasion, and sure enough, a couple of virus-spattering flying saucers and a humongous "robot orb" appear and wreak havoc. Meanwhile, Kenji's feisty niece Kanna and his best bud – the calm, cool, and collected Otcho – inspire the various anti-Friend factions to rise up. Be sure to stay tuned beyond the closing credits, when director Yukihiko Tsutsumi neatly ties up all the loose ends. D: Tsutsumi. C: Toshi Karasawa, Etsushi Toyokawa, Takako Tokiwa, Teruyuki Kagawa, Airi Taira, Hitomi Kuroki. 20TH CENTURY BOYS FILM PARTNERS

U

ULTRAMAN GAIA: THE BATTLE IN HYPERSPACE (J 1999, US 2002) **½ Wide-eyed tykes and nostalgic daikaiju buffs alike will get a bang out of this lively installment featuring the supersized superhero known as "Urutoraman" in his native Japan. Our friend from deep space established himself as a cultural sensation in his homeland even before the initial ULTRAMAN television series reached U.S. shores in the early 1970s via the UHF band. Similar to the enduring appeal of STAR TREK, the Ultraman saga continues to delight generation after generation. The action here moves quickly as nine-year-old Tsutomu finds a reddish glass ball with the power to grant wishes. He calls forth his idol, Agent Gamu of the XIG creature combat unit – who's also the alter ego of Ultraman Gaia. Trouble is, a remorseless school bully has snatched the glowing sphere and conjured up a nightmarish stable of gigantic rabble-rousers. Foremost is King of Mons, a foul-breathed reptile who shockingly spawns an additional pair of beastly bad boys: the extended-neck space monster Bajiris, and the swift ocean-dweller, Scylla. Gaia's interstellar associates, Ultraman Tiga and Ultraman Dyna, jump in near film's end to balance out the tussle. A boffo socko hit in Japan, even outgrossing the excellent GODZILLA 2000. D: Kazuya Konaka. C: Takeshi Yoshioka, Gaku Homada, Mai Saito, Sei Hiraizumi. TSUBURAYA PRODUCTIONS

ULTRAMAN GINGA S: THE MOVIE (J 2015, US 2017) ** Could this restless flick possibly be intended for those with attention-deficit disorder? I betcha. GINGA S flies out of the gate and doesn't let up for its frantic 63-minute duration. Not really old-school Ultraman here – it's influenced more by the Mighty Morphin Power Rangers. The Ultra Party Guardians, a contemporary version of the Science Patrol, seem fresh out of high school. How can these pikers – with their teenage idol looks – bear the weight of the world? Etelgar, a golden-toned giant creature with ram-like horns and an elegant scarf, is the latest threat; he enlists a warrior woman to help him imprison a bunch of Heisei Era Ultramen high in the sky. I can't keep 'em straight, though some fit into their rubber wetsuits better than others. Conspicuous, however, is the impatient Ultraman Zero, who's pretty dang funny. The Ultra dudes eventually escape and unite to confront the menace – a common motif in widescreen Ultra fare. I suppose this is what it is, but a little more moola in the budget would have kicked things up a notch. D: Koichi Sakamoto. C: Takuya Negishi, Kiyotaka Uji, Yukari Taki, Takahiro Katou, Ryuichi Oura. TSUBURAYA PRODUCTIONS/SHOCHIKU

ULTRAMAN: THE NEXT (J 2004, US 2005) *** Japan's venerable superhero from the cosmos gets a major overhaul in this eagerly-anticipated update, which vies to appeal to both lifelong fans and newer devotees. Purists may scoff at the U-Man's radical redesign; the big guy is now armored, predominantly silver and gray in hue, and more robotic. But hey, it's not that bad a look. Shinichi Maki (Tetsuya Bessho) is a jet pilot investigating an unidentified object over Tokyo when he is sucked into a spacious mass of colorful lights. Emerging unharmed, Shinichi soon realizes he has the capacity to transform into the mighty Ultraman. He's abducted by a hush-hush government agency and coerced to contend with a monstrous, morphing lizard that's causing turmoil. (The repugnant creature consumes crows and rats for energy.) The aerial exchange betwixt our adversaries – amidst blue sky, sun, and clouds – is a thing of beauty. Yuichi Kikuchi (GODZILLA, MOTHRA, KING GHIDORAH: GIANT MONSTERS ALL-OUT ATTACK; GODZILLA AGAINST MECHAGODZILLA) coordinated the effects, integrating CGI with suitmation, miniatures, and other tried-and-true traditional methods. The solid script focuses on the conflicted Shinichi, a military man whose responsibilities keep him apart from his wife and young son for lengthy stints of time. This fine pic had but a limited release in the States, with screenings at select film festivals. D: Kazuya Konaka. C: Bessho, Kyoko Konama, Kenya Osumi, Nae Yuuki, Ryohei Hirota. TSUBURAYA PRODUCTIONS

ULTRAMAN TIGA AND ULTRAMAN DYNA (J 1998, US 2002) **½ The casual tokusatsu follower might be surprised to learn that more than 20 Ultraman-themed TV series have graced the Japanese airwaves over the years. There's even been a perpetual output of theatrical releases, though TIGA AND DYNA is one of only a handful to be officially distributed stateside. Rest assured, the quirky appeal of the original ULTRAMAN is retained, though the recent inclusion of CGI has replaced some of the quaint effects techniques of yesteryear. Gregarious, easy-going Shin Asuka (Takeshi Tsuruno) is a member of the seven-person Super GUTS (Global Unlimited Task Squad) monster-fightin' outfit. When membranous aliens from the planet Monera threaten the planet, Shin takes on the guise of the laser-zingin' Ultraman Dyna. He faces, unflinchingly, a mishmash of far-out daikaiju. There's Geranda, a hideous flying fiend that Dyna encounters on the moon; Deathfacer is a mammoth robot with a Gatling gun for an arm; and Queen Monera is a tentacled abomination with a disgusting sac pouch. Tiga eventually enters the fracas, combining with Dyna for some audacious acrobatics. Kiddie kaiju fans will definitely groove on it. AKA: ULTRAMAN TIGA AND ULTRAMAN DYNA: THE WARRIORS OF THE LIGHTING

STAR. D: Kazuya Konaka. C: Tsuruno, Ryo Kinomoto, Mariya Yamada, Aya Sugimoto, Ryo Kinomoto, Toshikazu Fukawa. TSUBURAYA PRODUCTIONS

ULTRAMAN TIGA AND ULTRAMAN DYNA: THE WARRIORS OF THE LIGHTING STAR See ULTRAMAN TIGA AND ULTRAMAN DYNA

ULTRAMAN TIGA: THE FINAL ODYSSEY (J 2000, US 2005) **½ Numerous incarnations of the Ultraman character have raised the Beta Capsule high since the towering superhero's first appearance on the Japanese tube in 1966. The energetic Tiga, with his ability to change battle modes, is undeniably one of the more fascinating. Maintaining the momentum of the popular ULTRAMAN TIGA television series, this feature-length outing finds the Global Unlimited Task Squad (GUTS) venturing to a South Pacific island and unearthing three enormous stone statues. The danged things come alive, and oddly enough, resemble Ultraman brethren. Plus, they're freakin' evil. GUTS member Daigo Madoka (portrayed by J-pop star Hiroshi Nagano) transfigures into Ultraman Tiga to deal with these so-called "warriors of darkness." But there's a catch. Tiga was aligned with this troika of malcontents some 30,000 years earlier before he chose a righteous path. Will he be drawn back to the dark side? Premiered in the U.S. at an Ultraman film fest but that English dub has presumably been put on the shelf. D: Hiromitsu Muraishi. C: Nagano, Takami Yoshimoto, Mio Takagi, Shigeki Kagemaru. TSUBURAYA PRODUCTIONS

ULTRAMAN X: THE MOVIE (J 2016, US 2017) **1/2 Ultraman's 50th anniversary film has the current incarnation, Ultraman X, joining forces with Ultraman Tiga and the original Ultraman ("sha!'") for a throwdown with a trio of revulsive creatures. The trouble starts when an incendiary television reporter removes a stone orb from an ancient pyramid, releasing the giant monster Zaigorg from centuries of inertia. The club-handed, lumbar-spiked brute wastes little time in summoning his berserk buddies, Gorg Antlar and Gorg Fire Golza. They're fixin' to do some serious damage, so five other Ultra Warriors (the collective name for Ultramen) drop by to provide x-tra help. Ultraman X's costume is, surprisingly, a bit drab compared to the rest, but he utilizes all of the colors of the rainbow in his dazzling arsenal of attacks. Most of the Ultraman flicks are extensions of TV programs, with this one based on a 2015 series. It's what you might expect: gaudy and goofy. D: Kiyotaka Taguchi. C: Kensuke Takahashi, Akane Sakanoue, Yushiko Hosada, Ukyo Matsumoto. TSUBURAYA PRODUCTIONS/SHOCHIKU

ULTRAMAN ZEARTH (J 1996, US 2005) ** Imagine if Ultraman – Japan's iconic superhero from the far reaches of outer space – was unsure of himself, had an extreme dislike of dirt, and was not particularly adept at reining in his immense powers. That's the premise of ULTRAMAN ZEARTH, a kid-oriented parody of the Ultraman mythos. Katsuto, a klutzy service station attendant with a hygiene fixation, has the capability (sometimes) to turn into Ultraman Zearth by activating his electric toothbrush. When gold-pilfering aliens unleash a pair of giant monstrosities – a laser-zappin' horned lizard and a squidlike brain – Zearth musters up the courage to take 'em on. An ideal flick for those with short attention spans, as it breezes by in a snappy 51 minutes. Tough to find, though, as it was barely shown in the Western Hemisphere. Followed in 1997 by ULTRAMAN ZEARTH II. D: Shinya Nakajima. C: Misaharu Sekiguchi, Yuka Takaoka, Takaaki Ishibashi, Noritake Kinashi. TSUBURAYA PRODUCTIONS

V

VARAN THE UNBELIEVABLE (J 1958, US 1962) *½ He has been described as a "prehistoric bat" and a "mutated flying squirrel," but Varan, our spikey-spined title creature, is clearly a big ol,' butt-ugly lizard. Granted, the contemptible critter can soar with the best of 'em – but only if you're watching the Japanese version. Following the lead of 1956's GODZILLA, KING OF THE MONSTERS, this flick was drastically altered for the American market, with all airborne shots of Varan inexplicably removed. Scenes were added featuring Myron Healey (a recognizable mug in 1950s TV westerns) as a no-nonsense naval commander overseeing the experiments that awaken Varan from his deep siesta at the bottom of a lake. Military firepower ticks him off, and the grouchy behemoth heads, of course, to Tokyo. Serious daikaiju eiga fans will opt for the Japanese original (**½) as the film flows at a steadier pace. Akira Ifukube's majestic score is also kept intact. Incidentally, the last Toho sci-fi effort to be lensed in black-and-white. D: Ishiro Honda, Jerry Baerwitz. C: Healey, Kozo Nomura, Tsuruko Kobayashi, Ayumi Sonoda. TOHO

VIRUS (J 1980, US 1980) ** The most expensive production in Japanese film history at the time of its release, VIRUS disappointed at the box office but is nevertheless treasured by a small but dedicated gaggle of fans. MM88, a fast-multiplying microbe developed by the U.S. Army, is accidentally dispersed during a botched heist. Earth's population is wiped out, save for the 855 men and eight women assigned to a scientific research base in Antarctica – where it's too cold for the deadly bug to take hold. If things aren't bad enough, scientists discover that an impending earthquake is certain to trigger automatic nuclear strikes at strategic spots throughout the world, including – believe it or not – our survivors' South Pole location. A couple of brave souls (played by Masao Kusakari and Bo Svenson) race, by way of submarine, to Washington D.C. to deactivate the launch system. The lifeless city streets are inundated with corpses; it's a gruesome sight, and effectively eerie. Directed by the unpredictable Kinji Fukasaku (BATTLE ROYALE, THE GREEN SLIME, MESSAGE FROM SPACE) and adapted from the novel by esteemed sci-fi writer Sakyo Komatsu ("Sayonara Jupiter," "The Submersion of Japan"). The pic features a cast identifiable to American movie and TV audiences of the era: Chuck Connors, Glenn Ford, George Kennedy, Robert Vaughn, et al. AKA: DAY OF RESURRECTION, THE END. D: Fukasaku. C: Kusakari, Tsunehiko Watasi, Isao Natsuyagi, Shinichi "Sonny" Chiba, Ford, Kennedy, Olivia Hussey. KADOKAWA/TOKYO BROADCASTING SYSTEM

VOYAGE INTO SPACE (J 1967-68, US 1970) **½ Full-length feature gleaned from four episodes of the medulla-mangling JOHNNY SOKKO AND HIS FLYING ROBOT television series that captivated UHF viewers in the early 1970s. Those unfamiliar with the show may deem VOYAGE INTO SPACE the work of madmen. Kiddo secret agent Johnny Sokko (Mitsunobu Kaneko) directs the actions of an atomic-powered giant robot (named, appropriately, Giant Robot) by shouting instructions into a cutting-edge transmitter wristwatch. Just so happens that a cobalt-tinted alien squid, Emperor Guillotine, has set his sights on our fair planet, unleashing a half-dozen or so of the weirdest daikaiju ever put on film. Amongst the oddities: a floating eyeball, a lava-chucking vine, and a bowling ball that flattens everything in its path! Giant Robot triumphantly answers the call. Curiously resembling an Egyptian pharaoh, the metallic marvel is fortified with a mind-bending cache of weapons. (His potent fingertip missiles are much favored.) Meanwhile, Johnny and fellow agent Jerry Mano dodge bullets galore from Emperor Guillotine's "Gargoyle Gang," an outfit of bad guys sporting standard-issue black shades and "skull berets." It's one strange trip. Based on the manga by Mitsutero Yokoyama, creator of the early anime classic, GIGANTOR. D: Minoru Yamada. C: Kaneko, Akio Ito, Shozaburo Date, Yumiko Katayama, Tomomi Kuwabara, Hirohiko Sato. TOEI/TV ASAHI/AMERICAN INTERNATIONAL

W

WAR IN SPACE See THE WAR IN SPACE

WAR IN SPACE, THE (J 1977, US 1980) *** A special effects extravaganza, heavily motivated by the classic Toho flicks BATTLE IN OUTER SPACE, GORATH, and ATRAGON. Using the planet Venus as their main base, oddly-garbed invaders from a faraway galaxy stage a sneak attack on Earth's major cities. The United Nations Space Forces spring into action, putting the finishing touches on a magnificent intergalactic battleship, the Gohten. A pet project of the renowned Professor Takigawa, the versatile vessel is equipped with a rotating drill nose, depth-charge rockets, and revolver lasers. Our vaunted enemy counters with gumball-shaped flying saucers, and a stately space galleon with laser-shooting oars. The "explosive" finale, amidst the rugged terrain and shrouded atmosphere of Venus, is masterfully executed by visual effects man Teruyoshi Nakano. Unfortunately, this would be the last theatrical film directed by Jun Fukuda, helmsman of some of the more vivacious Godzilla efforts of the Showa Era. An obvious nod to STAR WARS: the inclusion of a yellow-horned, scythe-swinging Chewbacca stand-in as one of the heavies. AKA: WAR IN SPACE. D: Fukuda. C: Kensaku Morita, Ryo Ikebe, Yuko Asano, Hiroshi Miyauchi. TOHO

WAR OF THE GARGANTUAS (J 1966, US 1970) **½ Unusual tale of sibling rivalry gone awry, as a pair of bushy-haired Yeti of contrasting hues settle their differences in the Japanese countryside. Sanda, the brown one, was raised in captivity and is a pacifist at heart. Gaira, the green one, snacks on humans and is, well, outright ornery. The inevitable scuffle ensues. Unlike previous daikaiju eiga of the period, Japan's military forces are fairly effective; Jun Tazaki, in his customary role as a humorless general, is prominently featured. Don't worry – there's still a sufficient quota of toy tanks and helicopters obliterated to satisfy the most fervent of genre fans. Caught in the crossfire, the benevolent Sanda is defended by a laidback (or stoned?) American scientist (Russ Tamblyn) and his concerned lab assistant (Kumi Mizuno). (Yep, that's the same Russ Tamblyn who played Riff, sprightly leader of the Jets in WEST SIDE STORY.) Sort of a sequel to FRANKENSTEIN CONQUERS THE WORLD, though that's unclear in the dubbed U.S. release. A can't-miss scene: Songstress Kipp Hamilton literally brings down the house when her moving rendition of "Feel In My Throat" prompts the evil Gaira to crash a swank, rooftop nightclub. D: Ishiro Honda. C: Tamblyn, Mizuno, Kenji Sahara, Tazaki. TOHO

WAR OF THE INSECTS See GENOCIDE

WAR OF THE MONSTERS (J 1966, US 1967) ** Brrr! Gamera, the jet-powered giant turtle, gets a chilly reception (in this, his second feature film) from Barugon, "the quick-freeze monster." The gigantic gator-lizard dispenses a frosty mist from the tip of its projectile tongue, covering our hard-shelled hero with an icy coating. Gamera eventually thaws; thank goodness the rainbow-emitting Barugon has been kept in check by artificial rain. What the . . . ? Actually, this is pretty tame stuff as far as the Gamera sequels go. There's not even a small fry for the "children's pal" to save. Gamera still flies the friendly skies like a flying saucer on overdrive. Big show-off! Amid the monster mayhem, a sacred opal is filched from the natives of a tropical island by a big-time bad dude. That's never a good idea. AKA: GAMERA VS.

BARUGON. D: Shigeo Tanaka. C: Kojiro Hongo, Kyoko Enami, Yuzo Hayakawa, Takuya Fujioka. DAIEI

WARNING FROM SPACE (J 1956, US 1960) **½ This intelligent, underrated effort was the first Japanese sci-fi flick filmed in color. One-eyed starfish creatures show up in Tokyo to warn of a runaway planet on a collision course with Earth. Conveniently, our new alien friends – whose own world is also in peril – are experts in atomic energy; by working in unison, they reason, the rogue object can be blasted off path by our race's immense nuclear artillery. But they better get a move on. There's panic in the streets as the blazing ball of fire nears. The heat is stifling, and tidal waves are engulfing cities. Scripted by Kurosawa collaborator Hideo Oguni, the meticulously-paced story offers a pensive glimpse of urban life in mid-1950s Japan. The extraterrestrial starfish, essentially beige-tinged cloth stretched over extended human limbs, were designed by avant-garde artist Taro Okamoto. Unwary earthlings are understandably startled by their mere presence; to blend in, one of the intrepid echinoderms assumes the identity of a well-known nightclub singer. And this girl has got it goin' on: leaping 10 feet high to return tennis lobs, passing through solid doors, grasping complicated scientific formulas, etc. It's enough to make even a self-assured fella feel a bit insecure. D: Koji Shima. C: Keizo Kawasaki, Toyumi Karita, Bin Yagisawa, Shozu Nanbu. DAIEI

WHAT'S UP, TIGER LILY? (J 1965, US 1966) ***½ Woody Allen's directorial debut – of sorts – is this witty, irreverent spoof of espionage flicks. Allen inherited a sexy Japanese spy thriller called INTERNATIONAL SECRET

POLICE: KEY OF KEYS and dubbed in absurd, yet funny, English dialogue. Hence, a caper about missing microfilm is transformed into a preposterous quest for the world's best egg salad recipe. (As it's explained in the movie, the possessor of the stolen recipe will wield the power to rule the planet.) Adding to the insanity are frequent appearances by the Lovin' Spoonful, whose upbeat folk-rock tunes work the crowd into a frenzy at the local dance clubs. Those scenes were inserted without Allen's consent, but they're a nice touch. The original release, put out by Toho, is worth seeking out. The James Bond-ish lead role (known in Allen's version as Phil Moskowitz) is played by Tatsuya Mihashi with carefree charm and a bemused sense of humor. And the pic surprisingly succeeds without an abundance of gadgetry or flashy special effects. D: Allen, Senkichi Taniguchi. C: Mihashi, Akiko Wakabayashi, Mie Hama, Tadao Nakamaru, Susumu Kurobe, Eisei Amamoto, Kumi Mizuno, Tetsu Nakamura. BENEDICT PICTURES/TOHO

WORLD SINKS EXCEPT JAPAN, THE (J 2006, US 2007) **½ Outrageous take on disaster films, particularly JAPAN SINKS (2006) and 1973's SUBMERSION OF JAPAN. Moreover, it's a stark mad mockery of cross-cultural differences. It's the year 2011, and a combination of global warming and seismic shifts beneath the earth's crust sink the world's land mass into deep blue oblivion – except for Japan. Displaced foreigners – especially Americans – flock to the last piece of dry terrain on the planet but have difficulty assimilating to the Japanese way of life. It isn't long before the "gaijin" are considered troublesome outcasts. Director Minoru Kawasaki, known for oddball flicks like THE CALAMARI WRESTLER and MONSTER X

STRIKES BACK: ATTACK THE G8 SUMMIT, deliberately uses blatant stereotypes to make his point. (That's Kawasaki himself in the amusing "giant superhero" sequence.) Lunacy reigns supreme, and then – out of left field – a poignant, thought-provoking ending. Never woulda thunk it! D: Kawasaki. C: Kenji Kohashi, Shuji Kashiwabara, Masatoshi Matsuo. KLOCK WORX

WRATH OF DAIMAJIN See RETURN OF THE GIANT MAJIN

X

X FROM OUTER SPACE, THE (J 1967, US 1968) *** En route to Mars, the four enthusiastic crew members of the spaceship AAB Gamma stop by the moon for some well-deserved R&R and find a groovy, happenin' scene. Cocktails before dinner, anyone? How about a little dancing? Hot tubbing tonight? Unfortunately, it's a brief layover. Our cosmic trekkers resume their journey only to be bombarded by an unexpected meteor shower, and pestered by a UFO resembling an oversized apple fritter. The mission is scrapped, but the able adventurers secure a spore sample that attached itself to the spacecraft's hull. Back on Earth, the mysterious microorganism grows into the 15,000-ton, energy-absorbing monster Guilala. With its bird-like beak, orangish bug eyes, and oingy-boingy antennae, the anomalous Guilala would be right at home in an ULTRAMAN episode. Wonderfully quirky – even more so than most other daikaiju flicks. Taku Izumi's loungy music score bounces merrily along from start to finish. D: Kazui Nihonmatsu. C: Eiji Okada, Peggy Neal, Toshiya Wazaki, Itoko Hirada, Toshinori Kazusaki. SHOCHIKU

Y

YATTERMAN (J 2009, US 2009) *** Colorful, wacky live-action rendering of the popular 1970s anime series, with provocative director Takashi Miike at the helm. Toy shop employees Gan, a dude with stupendous mechanical aptitude, and Ai, his faithful female assistant, don masks and snazzy attire to fight the neverending forces of evil. They're aided by an libidinous mecha dog and a small-scale flying robot. Our heroes are quick to the fore when the skull-faced Dokurobe, a wannabe god, attempts to control the globe by harnessing the power of the coveted "skull stone." Dokurobe enlists the help of the nefarious Doronbo gang: the alluring Mistress Doronjo, the pig-nosed Tonzra, and the rat-faced Boyacky. Also in the melange is a giant, jet-propelled metal squid, and an automated gal with boob missiles. Miike interjects an ample amount of offbeat jocularity amidst the rapid-fire bustle. The Japanese title of the film – YATTAMAN – literally translates as, "We did it, man." D: Miike. C: Sho Sakurai, Saki Fukuda, Kyoko Fukada, Kendo Kobayashi, Katsuhisa Namase. YATTERMAN FILM PARTNERS

YOG, MONSTER FROM SPACE (J 1970, US 1971) **½ YOG sometimes gets a bad rap but it's an agreeable way for Japanese sci-fi fans to spend 90 minutes or so.

Widely regarded as the last film of Toho's classic era of daikaiju eiga, perhaps the expectations are unreasonably lofty. An unmanned space probe to Jupiter is infiltrated by a shimmery blue mist. The craft abruptly reverses course and crash-lands near a South Pacific isle, releasing alien microbes with the ability to unify with – and enlarge – other life forms. A squishy, giant-headed octopus (named Gezora) emerges; a few natives are promptly flung about and a village is trashed. Soon after, heightened versions of a pumice stone crab (Ganimes) and a snapping turtle (Kamoebas) enter the fray, courtesy of the glistening Yogsters. Meanwhile, a contingent of well-liked Toho players (including Akira Kubo in his last major genre role to date) provide the human element. AKA: SPACE AMOEBA. D: Ishiro Honda. C: Kubo, Atsuko Takahashi, Yoshio Tsuchiya, Kenji Sahara. TOHO

Z

ZEBRAMAN (J 2004, US 2007) *** Unforeseen offering from Takashi Miike, the controversial director of ICHI THE KILLER and IZO. Not averse to shocking audiences with unrestricted displays of graphic violence, Miike darn-near steers ZEBRAMAN into family-friendly territory. Shinichi Ichikawa, a disrespected teacher and family man, escapes the daily doldrums by wearing a homemade costume of his childhood idol, the daunting title character of the short-lived superhero show, ZEBRAMAN. Taking to the streets, an apprehensive Shinichi (a splendid performance from Show Aikawa) is unexpectedly bestowed with prodigious strength and agility. Good thing 'cause irksome monsters from the television series – obnoxious crab creatures and gooey-green aliens masquerading as humans – suddenly turn up. Realizing that the ZEBRAMAN program was actually a foretold prophecy, Shinichi slips into his black-and-white striped uni to battle the baddies. Miike deftly adds humor into the mix but there's tender moments, too. You can't help but root for our beleaguered protagonist, a down-and-out soul with a new lease on life. D: Miike. C: Aikawa, Kyuoko Suzuki, Naoki Yasukouchi, Atsuro Watabe. TOEI

ZEBRAMAN 2: ATTACK ON ZEBRA CITY (J 2010, US 2011) **½ Acclaimed director Takashi Miike follows up the much-admired ZEBRAMAN (2004) with this higher-financed, kookier sequel featuring Show Aikawa again as our resilent, banded hero. It's the year 2025, and Tokyo – now dubbed Zebra City – is in upheaval. The Zebra Queen, a flamboyant pop music diva in skin-tight black, has instituted "Zebra Time," a 10-minute period each day when the police can freely murder citizens presumed to be criminals. Shinichi Ichikawa – a.k.a. Zebraman – is a shadow of his former self. Just 15 years prior, he saved Earth from extraterrestrial intruders. But the poor guy has lost his memory and had his superpowers usurped. With the help of both a young protégé and the actor who portrays Zebraman on television, Shinichi gradually discovers his past persona and vows to make things right. The film's frantic finish, with Zebraman taking on a massive, green CGI blob, is pure insanity. Riisa Naka, terrific as the lead in THE GIRL WHO LEAPT THROUGH TIME, won the Japanese Film Academy Award for her turn as the diabolical Zebra Queen. D: Miike.

C: Aikawa, Naka, Tsuyoshi Abe, Masahiro Inoue, Noaki Tanaka, Mei Nakano, Makie Amamoto. TOEI/CENTRAL ARTS/TOKYO BROADCASTING SYSTEM

ZEIRAM (J 1991, US 1994) *** Wildly entertaining thriller from the fertile mind of director Keita Amemiya. Zeiram, an 8-foot-tall, genetically-engineered nightmare from a distant world, brutally offs his keepers and flees to Earth. Hot on the heels is female bounty hunter Iria (Yuko Moriyama) and her partner, a worrywart computer named Bob. Exceptionally skilled and brimming with confidence, Iria expects a quick capture. The Big Z, however, is something else. His mushroom-shaped noggin houses a retractable appendage with a tiny human head (resembling the white-faced Noh of Japanese theater) that viciously strikes out to suck the genetic material from living beings. Stumbling into the thick of things is a pair of likeable goofballs, Kamiya and Teppei. (Kamiya is played by Yukijiro Hotaru, the bewildered police investigator in GAMERA: GUARDIAN OF THE UNIVERSE.) One of Amemiya's early efforts but certainly representative of his singular style, with brisk pacing, imaginative special effects, and surprising visuals. Followed by the equally impressive ZEIRAM II. AKA: ZERAM. D: Amemiya. C: Moriyama, Hotaru, Kunihiko Ida. CROWD/GAGA

ZEIRAM II (J 1994, US 2001) *** This follow-up to 1991's ZEIRAM is just as lively and immoderate as its predecessor – and a heckuva lot of fun. Iria, bounty hunter babe from outer space, returns to Earth to locate a mystical relic and bumps into old foe Zeiram, an unusual humanoid with a mind-blowing array of sophisticated weaponry and a serious mean streak. Director Keita Amemiya again puts the pedal to the metal as the adroit adversaries engage in a number of intense, well-executed tussles. Back from the first pic to assist Iria are Bob the talking computer, and the bumbling yet brave duo of Kamiya and Teppei, a couple of ordinary guys who provide comic respite during the film's heavier stretches. Yet unexplained is the weird miniature head that protrudes from Zeiram when the creature requires sustenance. An unsuspecting pooch is in the wrong place at the wrong time, spawning a canine aberration that would send Cujo scampering home with its tail between its legs. AKA: ZERAM II. D: Amemiya. C: Yuko Moriyama, Yukijiro Hotaru, Kunihiko Ida. CROWD/ZEIRAM PROJECT

ZERAM See ZEIRAM

ZERAM II See ZEIRAM II

TALK THE TALK

What the heck is tokusatsu? And what in tarnation is a daikaiju? Peruse the list below and you'll be well on your way to becoming a bona fide kaiju eiga expert.

anime: A colorful, distinctive style of animation originating from Japan. Derived from **manga**.

CGI (Computer-Generated Imagery): The utilization of computer graphics to create high-quality special effects for motion pictures.

cyberpunk: Unique sci-fi film genre featuring abnormal use of technology in chaotic, urbanized settings.

Daiei: The film company that brought us Gamera, Majin, and Zatoichi, the blind swordsman. Started in 1942, Daiei declared bankruptcy in 1971, was revived a few years later, and was then bought out by Kadokawa in 2002.

daikaiju: Westerners translate this Japanese word as "giant monster."

daikaiju eiga: Giant monster movies from Japan.

dubbing: Providing a film with substitute dialogue. Japanese sci-fi flicks are dubbed into English for our rabid consumption.

eiga: Japanese term for cinema, film, movies, etc.

FX: Catchy abbreviation for special effects. See also **SFX, SPFX, VFX**.

gaijin: A non-Japanese person, usually Caucasian.

Heisei Era: Japanese monster movies from the 1980s and 1990s; ranges from GODZILLA 1985 (J 1984) to GAMERA: THE REVENGE OF IRIS (J 1999).

Honda, Ishiro (1911-1993)**:** Director of GOJIRA and several other Toho sci-fi classics. A gentle, peaceful man, his films often expressed a humanistic point of view.

Ifukube, Akira (1914-2006)**:** Classical music composer best known for his work in Godzilla films and other kaiju eiga. Godzilla's recognizable march theme is typical of Ifukube's style: heavy, melodic, and grandiose.

J-pop: Japanese pop music.

kaijin: Basically, the individuals in a state of flux in pics like H-MAN, THE HUMAN VAPOR, and SECRET OF THE TELEGIAN; means "mysterious person" in Japanese.

kaiju: Literally, "mysterious beast" or "strange beast" but the Yankee interpretation is "monster."

kaiju eiga: Monster movie.

katana: Type of sword used by feudal era samurai.

manga: Japanese comic art known for its visually-dynamic style; read from right-to-left and usually published in black-and-white.

mecha: An armored combat vehicle, often in robotic form, that walks and is typically piloted by humans.

Millenium Era: Any Japanese monster movie released from the year 2000-on. Also known as the Shinsei Era.

miniatures: Division of special effects utilizing scale models (cars, tanks, planes, submarines, buildings, etc.).

Nakajima, Haruo (1929-2017)**:** Suit actor who enthusiastically wedged himself into Godzilla's latex garb – and that of various other kaiju – from 1954-1972. He often performed under difficult, hazardous conditions.

SFX: Another catchy abbreviation for special effects. See also **FX, SPFX, VFX**.

Shinsei Era: "Rebirth" or "new beginning," it's an alternate name for the Millenium Era.

SPFX: Yet another catchy abbreviation for special effects. See also **FX, SFX, VFX**.

Showa Era: Japanese monster films made during the period of history corresponding with the reign of Emperor Showa; ranges from the 1954 release of GOJIRA (AKA: GODZILLA, KING OF THE MONSTERS) to the 1980 production of GAMERA: SUPER MONSTER.

stop-motion photography: Special effects technique where an object is moved in small increments and photographed one frame at a time to make the object appear as though it's moving on its own.

subtitles: Printed translation of foreign film dialogue, with the text displayed at the bottom of the screen.

suitmation: Originally developed by special effects innovator Eiji Tsuburaya to portray Godzilla; it's the art of using an actor in a rubber suit to play a giant monster.

Tanaka, Tomoyuki (1910-1997)**:** Toho producer who dreamt up the idea of Godzilla. Besides kaiju eiga, Tanaka also produced war and crime films for the company, along with epic works from Akira Kurosawa.

Toho: Motion picture studio located in Tokyo that has given us Godzilla, Mothra, Rodan, King Ghidorah, and numerous other unforgettable kaiju. Established in 1932, Toho has always dabbled in a variety of genres.

Toho's golden age: The stretch of time from 1954-1970, when Toho Studios released a steady output of much-loved daikaiju eiga and tokusatsu films. Both the actors and production personnel remained somewhat constant throughout this highly-creative period.

tokusatsu: Refers to films or TV shows (especially those of the superhero ilk) using expansive special effects – or to the special effects themselves.

Tsuburaya, Eiji (1901-1970)**:** The father of Japanese special effects, Tsuburaya (and a crew of 60) cleverly combined suitmation, the use of detailed miniatures, the detonation of carefully-rigged explosives, and groundbreaking optical techniques to provide Toho monster films with an inimitable look and feel.

Tsuburaya Productions: Company founded in 1963 by Toho's visionary special effects director, Eiji Tsuburaya. Created a niche with science-fiction television series like ULTRA Q, ULTRAMAN, and MIGHTY JACK, and eventually branched out into big-screen fare.

UHF (Ultra High Frequency): Television band, featuring independently-run stations, that started catching steam in the U.S. in the 1970s. Needing programming, Japanese sci-fi movies were regularly aired.

VFX: What? One more abbreviation for special effects? Whoa. See also **FX, SFX, SPFX**.

ORDERING INFO

TOKUSATSU, TRANSMUTATIONS, AND TITANS: AN A-Z GUIDE TO JAPANESE SCI-FI FILMS is available at Amazon.com.

ABOUT THE AUTHOR

George Cervenka Jr. is a former sports and entertainment writer for the Geauga Times Leader newspaper. He currently works for the Geauga County Board of Developmental Disabilities. He lives in Reminderville, Ohio with his wife Kelly, and daughters Eve and Mia. This is his first book.